An Introduction to Some Unanswered Questions in Christendom

Vol. 1

*A Practical View on Christianity and
A Guide for Newly Converted Believers*

By

Francis Obed Fornah (PhD)

An Introduction to Some Unanswered Questions in Christendom

Copyright © 2020 by **Francis Obed Fornah (PhD)**.
All rights reserved.
Requests for information should be addressed to:
graceministries2017@gmail.com

This book, or parts thereof, may not be reproduced, stored in a retrieval system, or transmitted in any form or by any means, electronic, mechanical, photocopying, recording or otherwise, without the written permission of the publisher.

Published By: **Achievers World Publishing, Australia.**

ISBN: 978-0-6485985-0-3 (Paperback)
ISBN: 978-0-6487534-7-6 (ebook)

Unless otherwise stated, Scripture quotations are from the New King James Version (NKJV) of the Bible.

Printed in Australia

Dedication

As we all strive to understand the kind of faith we have and the prices we pay for such belief, I have therefore dedicated this handpiece of work to you reading this book for the courage you have taken to do so. Secondly to God who gave me the knowledge, wisdom and understanding and finally to my wife who taught me to be patient and tolerant.

Acknowledgement

In a world of researchers and writers, we see how we are surrounded by GOD's fantastic craftsmanship which shows drastic evidence of His existence by creating people filled with his knowledge, wisdom and understanding. People whose written words have gone all over the earth. **(Psalms 19 verses 1-4).** To this end, I feel really privileged and obliged to thank the Lord Jesus for what he has done in my life. He took me from zero to hero. He gave me the anointing to redeem the captive and set them free from the affluence and influence of Satan, whose aim is to steal, destroy and kill.

The following people also deserve to be acknowledged and given special thanks for being my mentors and spiritual guardians. Dr Bob Chapman, the author of Extreme lives for extreme times. Your encouragement and counselling gave me the zeal to follow your footsteps. As my lecturer, you saw in me the giftings that make a good author. Mr & Mrs Pearson, my Spiritual parents who have always been there to guide and direct me. Receiving a certificate from you for completing a rigorous study of the New Testament at your training sessions was an experience I will never forget.

God said it was not good for man to be alone. He created a companion for him that would live life by his side. A woman's role in a marriage is to honour that God ordained covenant. To my beloved wife Mrs Elizabeth Obed Fornah, for giving me the push and courage to complete this book. You are a true mentor who always cares for your husband. For every successful man, there is a progressive woman and you are one of those. Proverbs 1: 10-12 says: "A wife of noble character who can find? She is worth far more than rubies. Her husband has full confidence in her and lacks nothing of value. She brings him good, not harm, all the days of her life."

Dr Francis Fornah

Foreward

It is indeed a privilege to write this forward, not only because Dr Francis Fornah is my husband but also because I get to see him live out his faith every day. Authentic, bold, challenging and timely are just a few words that describe this book. We are living in a time when information is rife but we still have lots of questions because we are truth-seekers by nature.

Unanswered questions in Christendom is an easy read for believers and non-believers alike needing answers to both easy and hard and sometimes controversial questions. This book will ask, then attempt to answer questions based on the authority of the word of God. Dr Francis has been a seeker of truth from the word of God, his work is a reflection of his inquisitive nature and has been birthed to help believers not only get answers but also be challenged to think more. Didn't God tell us to love Him with all our minds? This book will definitely get you thinking.

The Scriptures (in Jude 3) encourage us to contend earnestly for the faith. Jesus Christ never shied away from the difficult questions that His disciples asked, even the questions from the Pharisees whose intent was to challenge His authority. Even when we can't seem to find easy answers, we know that in Christ Jesus we have all the Truth we need.

May this book be a blessing to all its readers in Jesus name.

Elizabeth A. Fornah

Statement of Service Value

"Do nothing out of selfish ambition or vain conceit. Rather, in humility value others above yourselves, not looking to your own interests but each of you to the interests of the others" (Philippians 2:3-4).

This is so because:

As we all strive to understand the kind of faith we have and the prices we pay for our beliefs, let us therefore "Be kindly affectionate one to another with brotherly love; in honour preferring one another;" - Romans 12:10

CONTENTS

Dedication iii

Acknowledgement iv

Foreward vi

Statement of Service Value vii

Introduction 1

Chapter 1: The Church and Christians (?) 3

   1.1 Are all church-goers Christians? 3

   1.2 Why is the church full of hypocrites and false prophets today? 8

   1.3 Is there a remedy for hypocrisy in the churches today? 18

Chapter 2: Christianity and Religion 22

   2.1 Why do Christians go through trials? 22

   2.2. If the God we are following is that powerful, why does He allow evil or bad things to happen to good people? 36

   2.3 Religion: When a Muslim criticizes Jesus, it's no offence but when a Christian does criticize Mohamed or Islam, it becomes a world issue. Why? 44

Chapter 3: The Ministry of Jesus vs. the Ministry of Men 52

   3.1 If the body of Christ is one, why are there so many churches doing different things in the name of Jesus? 54

3.2 Does it feel like churches are empty and the spiritual paddocks are bare? 59

Chapter 4: How Do We Honour And Respect Our Elders, Including Our Pastors? 66

Chapter 5: What Are Vanity and Eternity? 76

5.1 Can possession and pride lead us to eternity? 86

5.2 Who do you allow to define your identity and self-image? 94

Chapter 6: Church Hoppers and Prophecy Shoppers 113

Chapter 7: Understanding the Anointing 123

7.1 Do Witches Have Anointing Oil? 132

Chapter 8: What Does the Bible Teach Us About Giving? 139

Introduction

I am convinced a lot of writers have done their very best to answer some unexpected questions relating to the Christian faith we profess. Trust me; most of the answers they have given do not satisfy the people who asked. I am not immune to that fact.

This book is an introductory outline of my quest to research some unanswered questions in Christendom that have raised concerns in the lives of many families who have left churches. Some have departed because the pastors could not give them the answers they want; the church they call home betrayed their trust or the church and or the pastor has shifted from prototype to stereotype. Others have left because the church no longer preaches the gospel of Jesus. Instead, it compromises the Word of God for the word of men.

In some instances, the exodus from the church occurred because people are rebellious, disobedient, drinking from different spiritual wells and sometimes, flouting the authority of the church and its leadership.

The questions and answers contained in this book have been sent in by people who have been longing for the gospel of truth. The answers have been thoroughly researched and or contributed by other writers and spiritual leaders. May the Lord bless you as you read.

Note: Volume 2 of this book will follow soon after this one is published. It will examine critical issues related to what life is like in the Diaspora without Jesus. Believers who a done deal for Yeshua will be contacted to respond to some of these questions.

CHAPTER 1

The Church and Christians (?)

As believers, we all know the church is not the building. The word "church" comes from the Greek word *ekklesia*, which is defined as "an assembly" or the "called-out ones. So who are the called-out ones? Are these the worshipers in the church? Are these people called Christians? To find the answer to these questions, we will examine the book of Acts. The book of Acts was purposely written by Luke the physician to give an accurate account of the birth and growth of the Christian church.

> They all met together constantly in prayer, along with the women and Mary the mother of Jesus, and with his brothers. In those days Peter stood up among the believers (a group numbering about a hundred and twenty. (Acts 1:14-15 [1])

1.1 Are all church-goers Christians?

The answer to this question is no. In those days, the men and women who accompanied the apostles while Jesus was carrying out His Father's

---

[1] The book of Acts 1:14-15 "the growth of the Christian Church" (NIV)

work (as described in the first chapters of the Acts of the Apostles), were all Jews by birth or conversion. These people were united in spirit and had one goal, which was to spread the gospel of Jesus. However, most churches today are filled with hypocrites whose main objective is to seek self-righteousness or mount and nurse schools of gossipers, and slanderers who go the mile to offend other people or faithful worshippers.

Gossip, slander and offence are the three sins the Devil has successfully planted inside churches where the power of the Holy Spirit was once manifested. The Devil uses the very church members who are weak, occasional prayer warriors to inject them with one or all of these three sins or viruses. They immediately spread to others whom they can convince using the most powerful means called "Human Conversation." Human conversation is a potent tool. It can also be a very destructive weapon. How we use human language is a decision we make every day of our lives. What you say and the way you say it can be very creative or counterproductive.

In the New Testament book of James, the author warns about becoming a teacher. In other words, James [2] says, we must be very careful how we speak.

---

[2] James Chapter 3:1-2 of the Holy Bible (NIV)

> Do not let many of you become teachers. Knowing that as such we shall incur a stricter judgment. For we all stumble in many ways. If anyone does not stumble in what he says he is perfectly able to bridle the whole body as well. (James 3:1-2)

Many people who want to serve the Lord faithfully and their potential have been destroyed through gossip, slander, and offence. But what does the leadership in these churches do to correct such malpractices? This is a million-dollar question because some of these very leaders support the people who carry the virus.

The Word of God clearly states in many chapters that death and life are in the power of the tongue (Proverbs 18:21 and Isaiah 59). [3]

> Behold the Lord's hand is not shortened that it cannot save, nor his ear heavy that it cannot hear. But your iniquities have separated them from God: and your sins have hidden his face from you, so that he will not hear. For your hands are defiled with blood and your fingers with iniquity; your lips have spoken lies, your tongue has muttered perversity. (Isaiah 59:1-3)

We must understand how words affect our lives. You did what you did because you said what you said.

---

[3] The book of Proverbs and the book of Isaiah 59 (NIV)

These six things the Lord hates, yes, seven are an abomination to Him: verse 17 "A proud look, a lying tongue, hands that shed innocent blood. 18; A heart that devises wicked plans, feet that are swift in running to evil, 19; a false witness who speaks lies and one who sows discord among brethren. (Proverbs 6:16-19)

In that scripture, three out of the seven things God hates have to do with the mouth. People in modern-day churches go the mile to poke their noses into knowing other people's business and make that a spectacle. They do so instead of helping falling brothers or sisters who might be struggling with coping mechanisms or life-threatening problems that just need simple prayers. They find pleasure building their own stories and coming to their own conclusions about a situation or problem they don't even know about. They have no idea of its origin.

Proverbs 12:22 says, "Lying lips are an abomination to the Lord, but those who deal truthfully are his delight." To be called a Christian, you must be Christlike. Jesus Christ was a forthright preacher who called things by their names. If you are caught up in such practices, repent and ask for forgiveness. Then turn away from your evil ways. 2 Chronicles 7:14 very clearly said; "If my people, who are called by my name, will humble themselves and pray and seek my face and turn from their wicked ways, then I will hear from heaven, and I will forgive their sin and will heal their land" (NIV).

People go to church for several reasons as listed below:

1. To show-off

2. For social interaction because they are lonely

3. They hear that a powerful man of God has come and they want a quick fix to their problems

4. They want to drink from different wells (to find where the gospel is preached and if that does not suit them, they leave and go somewhere else. These are church hoppers and prophecy shoppers)

5. In search of places they call home

6. For spiritual guardians and or to grow spiritually

7. Looking for like-minded people who enter churches to see its downfall

The list goes on and on.

As a disciple of Christ, I would like to further answer this question by referring to what Dr. Natanael Costea [4] said in his book, *Forty Years and*

---

[4] Dr. Nathanael Costea *Forty Years and Forty Days* a book that talks about how God will reveal himself to you if you draw near to Him"

Forty Days about our daily cross-bearing. To be called a Christian is to deny yourself. He said:

> Self-denial is not denial of self. It relies on your own efforts and your works. It is seeking to be spiritually aligned with Christ no matter how much it cost. Secondly, it is to take up the cross of Jesus daily.

He further said and as we all know, "To bear the cross means death." Attending church without those qualities renders the purpose of going to church meaningless (*Forty Years and Forty Days* p110-111). Be a Christian, not a church-goer. Believe in Jesus Christ and nothing else. No plan "B."

1.2 Why is the church full of hypocrites and false prophets today?

I tried to research this topic to find the answer. However, I relied on the Holy Spirit, consulted a few godly men and came to this conclusion. A hypocrite is a person who puts on a mask and pretends to be who he or she is not. Hypocrites claim to know and follow certain beliefs, but they behave in ways that are contradictory to what they say. There is no perfect church in the 21st century. Most churches today have turned away from teaching and preaching the gospel of Jesus Christ. Instead, they are busy preaching the gospel of men.

Truly speaking, the Bible made it very clear that pastors and church leaders or elders are expected to be qualified:

Qualifications for Overseers and Deacons

> Here is a trustworthy saying: Whoever aspires to be an overseer desires a noble task. 2 Now the overseer is to be above reproach, faithful to his wife, temperate, self-controlled, respectable, hospitable, able to teach, 3 not given to drunkenness, not violent but gentle, not quarrelsome, not a lover of money. 4 He must manage his own family well and see that his children obey him, and he must do so in a manner worthy of full[a] respect. 5 (If anyone does not know how to manage his own family, how can he take care of God's church?) 6 He must not be a recent convert, or he may become conceited and fall under the same judgment as the devil. 7 He must also have a good reputation with outsiders, so that he will not fall into disgrace and into the devil's trap. 8 In the same way, deacons[b] are to be worthy of respect, sincere, not indulging in much wine, and not pursuing dishonest gain. 9 They must keep hold of the deep truths of the faith with a clear conscience. 10 They must first be tested; and then if there is nothing against them, let them serve as deacon. (1 Timothy 3:1-10)

Pastors and elders who are properly scrutinized cannot quickly jump the bandwagon to become hypocrites or false prophets without being challenged. Pastors and church elders must be respected and honored but not worshipped. Most African believers today have been caught up in the trap of worshipping their pastors or prophets more than their God, husbands, and wives. If you are one of those people who bow down to humans, I am referring to you. Stop it! These men of God are humans like you. They did not die on the cross for you. Their blood did not pay the price for your salvation.

Read your Bible very carefully. I tend to blame some of you for making these men and women of God pompous. Some of them had humble beginnings but as time went on, self-glory, self-pride and the hunger for fame cropped in. They have become immersed in the lust of the flesh:

> 16 For everything in the world—the lust of the flesh, the lust of the eyes, and the pride of life—comes not from the Father but from the world. (1 John 2:16)

Many of the congregations under the leadership of these ministers are subjected to financial stress, duress, and anxiety. Consequently, there is mental illness, which is a curse and demonic suppression. Scripture is clear-cut on such oppressive behaviours. Read it for free. We should have wisdom to discern the words and actions that do not match. We should also remember that God is the ultimate judge of character. Be very careful not to draw conclusions. The following scriptures will help to guide us:

> Do not judge, or you too will be judged. [2]For in the same way you judge others, you will be judged, and with the measure you use, it will be measured to you. [3]"Why do you look at the speck of sawdust in your brother's eye and pay no attention to the plank in your own eye? [4]How can you say to your brother, 'Let me take the speck out of your eye,' when all the time there is a plank in your own eye? [5]You hypocrite, first take the plank out of your own eye, and then you will see clearly to remove the speck from your brother's eye. (Matthew 7:1-5, NIV)

You, therefore, have no excuse, you who pass judgment on someone else, for at whatever point you judge another, you are condemning yourself, because you who pass judgment do the same things. [2]Now we know that God's judgment against those who do such things is based on truth. [3]So when you, a mere human being, pass judgment on them and yet do the same things, do you think you will escape God's judgment? [4]Or do you show contempt for the riches of his kindness, forbearance and patience, not realizing that God's kindness is intended to lead you to repentance? [5]But because of your stubbornness and your unrepentant heart, you are storing up wrath against yourself for the day of God's wrath, when his righteous judgment will be revealed. (Romans 2:1-5, NIV)[5]

Now, let us carefully examine these scriptures and begin to decipher what the writers were portraying. In Matthew 7:1-5, Jesus Himself tells us to examine our reasons and conduct before we start pointing fingers at others. The traits or habits that bother us in other people's lives are often the habits we portray or exhibit ourselves. Our bad habits and behavioural patterns are the very ones we want to change in others. Jesus warned us to stop judging others because hypocritical judgmental attitudes tear down the lives of people. We sometimes do this to build or justify ourselves.

In Romans 2:1-5, apostle Paul wrote to the Christians in Rome and believers all over the world. He counselled that whenever we find ourselves justifiably or unjustifiably angry about another person's character or behaviour, we should be very careful how we approach them about what we perceive to be sin. We must exercise humility and avoid judgment before knowing the cause. People all over the world today condemn others for sins they themselves commit.

If we look closely at ourselves, we may find that we are committing the same sins in a more serious but socially acceptable form. A typical

---

[5] In the book of Romans 2, 1-5 Paul reminded the Romans about judging others and putting up with one another.

example may be people who gossip. They may be critical or angry because others gossip about them. In spite of what you may perceive, be careful not to call people hypocrites when you are found wanting. As the saying goes, "When you live in a glass house, you should not throw stones." Yes, there are hypocrites and false prophets in and out of the church.

Let us examine a few scriptures in the Bible and glimpse at what they say about false prophets and teachers.

> But there were also false prophets among the people, just as there will be false teachers among you. They will secretly introduce destructive heresies, even denying the sovereign Lord who bought them—bringing swift destruction on themselves. [2] Many will follow their depraved conduct and will bring the way of truth into disrepute. [3] In their greed these teachers will exploit you with fabricated stories. Their condemnation has long been hanging over them, and their destruction has not been sleeping. [4] For if God did not spare angels when they sinned, but sent them to hell,[a] putting them in chains of darkness[b] to be held for judgment; [5] if he did not spare the ancient world when he brought the flood on its ungodly people, but protected Noah, a preacher of righteousness, and seven others; [6] if he condemned the cities of Sodom and Gomorrah by burning them to ashes, and made them an example of what is going to happen to the

ungodly; ⁷ and if he rescued Lot, a righteous man, who was distressed by the depraved conduct of the lawless ⁸ (for that righteous man, living among them day after day, was tormented in his righteous soul by the lawless deeds he saw and heard)— ⁹ if this is so, then the Lord knows how to rescue the godly from trials and to hold the unrighteous for punishment on the day of judgment. ¹⁰ This is especially true of those who follow the corrupt desire of the flesh[and despise authority. (2 Peter 2:1-10, NIV)

The Bible further said such people are bold and arrogant. They are not afraid to heap abuse on celestial beings. Peter was writing this to suffering Christians as a form of encouragement when the great persecution under Emperor Nero Hegan was in effect. It was his last letter before his execution.

Peter repeated what Jesus told His disciples about the coming of false prophets (see Matthew 24:11 and Mark 13:22-23). Peter had heard these words and saw that they were becoming a reality. In the Old Testament, false prophets often contradicted the true prophets of God (see Jeremiah 23:16-40 and Jeremiah 28:1-17). Let us look at these scriptures quickly and put our thoughts together for a second.

The prophet Jeremiah was commissioned to tell God's people to turn from their sins and come back to God. This message was for the people of the southern kingdom of Judah who were busy listening to other prophets.

> This is what the Lord Almighty says: "Do not listen to what the prophets are prophesying to you; they fill you with false hopes. They speak visions from their own minds, not from the mouth of the Lord. They keep saying to those who despise me, that the Lord says; You will have peace and to all those who follow the stubbornness of their hearts they say; No harm will come to you But which of them has stood in the council of the Lord to see or to hear his word? Who has listened and heard his word? [19] See, the storm of the Lord will burst out in wrath, a whirlwind swirling down on the heads of the wicked. [20] The anger of the Lord will not turn back until he fully accomplishes the purposes of his heart. In days to come you will understand it clearly. I did not send these prophets, yet they have run with their message; I did not speak to them, yet they have prophesied.
>
> But if they had stood in my council, they would have proclaimed my words to my people and would have turned them from their evil ways and from their evil deeds. "Am I only a God nearby," declares the Lord, "and not a God far away? Who can hide in secret places so that I cannot see them?" declares the Lord. "Do not I fill heaven and earth?" declares the Lord. "I have heard what the prophets say who prophesy lies in my name. They say, 'I had a dream! I had a dream!'

How long will this continue in the hearts of these lying prophets, who prophesy the delusions of their own minds? They think the dreams they tell one another will make my people forget my name, just as their ancestors forgot my name through Baal worship. Let the prophet who has a dream recount the dream, but let the one who has my word speak it faithfully. For what has straw to do with grain?" declares the Lord. "Is not my word like fire," declares the Lord, "and like a hammer that breaks a rock in pieces? "Therefore," declares the Lord, "I am against the prophets who steal from one another words supposedly from me. Yes," declares the Lord, "I am against the prophets who wag their own tongues and yet declare, 'The Lord declares.' **32** Indeed, I am against those who prophesy false dreams," declares the Lord. "They tell them and lead my people astray with their reckless lies, yet I did not send or appoint them. They do not benefit these people in the least," declares the Lord.

[False Prophecy]

"When these people, or a prophet or a priest, ask you, 'What is the message from the Lord?' say to them, 'What message? I will forsake you, declares the Lord.' If a prophet or a priest or anyone else claims, 'This is a message from the Lord,' I will punish them and their household. **35** This is what each of you keeps saying to your friends and other Israelites: 'What is the Lord's answer?' or 'What has the

Lord spoken?' But you must not mention 'a message from the Lord' again, because each one's word becomes their own message. So, you distort the words of the living God, the Lord Almighty, our God. This is what you keep saying to a prophet: 'What is the Lord's answer to you?' or 'What has the Lord spoken?' Although you claim, 'This is a message from the Lord,' this is what the Lord says: You used the words, 'This is a message from the Lord,' even though I told you that you must not claim, 'This is a message from the Lord.' Therefore, I will surely forget you and cast you out of my presence along with the city I gave to you and your ancestors. I will bring on you everlasting disgrace—everlasting shame that will not be forgotten. (Jeremiah 23:16-40, NIV)

True prophets and false prophets are as different as chaff and wheat. Chaff is useless for food, while wheat is so nourishing, it cannot be compared to chaff. True prophets are the wheat and false prophets are the chaff. Sharing the gospel is a great responsibility because the way we present it will encourage people to accept or reject it. Whether we speak from a pulpit, teach in a theological school or share with friends, we must accurately present it in a way that shows that we are living God's Word.

As you share God's Word with people, others will also watch. They will observe whether you are living the Word you preach and its effectiveness in you. Unless the same word you preach has changed you, don't expect them to believe that it will change them. Therefore, you must rebuke and correct prophets who tell you to do things that are not biblical. Don't just dance to the tune of prophets because they carry a title. Corroborate every word they say with the Word of God.

1.3 Is there a remedy for hypocrisy in the churches today?

Yes, there is. Many church goers today call themselves Christians, but they do not follow the likeness of Jesus. Actually, they have made a way for Satan to enter many churches and destabilize the foundation on which each church was built.

The first remedy for hypocrites is prayer. You must pray for them because such people may also carry the spirit of Jezebel and Ahab. But again, let us look at a few aspects of those Christians we call hypocrites.

Ken Palmer [6] a lay preacher at Life of Christ Ministries said in his article published on February 2007 whilst responding to Kevin Flahaut's blog, "Kevin, you remind me of the old quote, 'If a hypocrite is standing between you and God, who is closer to God?'" Seriously, look at the Corinthian church or the seven churches in Asia Minor in the book of Revelations. They all had problems. They were full of people who made mistakes. Even the apostle Paul struggled with sin (Romans 7:22-24). Did that make him a hypocrite or was he human? That's one reason forgiveness is so

---

[6] Ken Palmer (2007); Who knows who will read this. Hypocrites?

important. We all stand in need of forgiveness, and we all need to have forgiving spirits.

Jesus said, "For if you forgive men when they sin against you, your heavenly Father will also forgive you. But if you do not forgive men their sins, your Father will not forgive your sins" (Matthew 6:14-15). None of us are perfect. "For all have sinned and fall short of the glory of God" (Romans 3:23). If we were all perfect, then we wouldn't need Christ's sacrifice. John wrote about the human struggle against sin:

> If we say that we have fellowship with Him and yet walk in the darkness, we lie and do not practice the truth; but if we walk in the Light as He Himself is in the Light, we have fellowship with one another, and the blood of Jesus His Son cleanses us from all sin. If we say that we have no sin, we are deceiving ourselves and the truth is not in us. If we confess our sins, He is faithful and righteous to forgive us our sins and to cleanse us from all unrighteousness. If we say that we have not sinned, we make Him a liar and His word is not in us. (1 John 1:5-10)

Even the best Christians sin. But John's point is that our lifestyles, attitudes, and humility—not a single action—define our relationship with God. That's what walking in the light refers to. If a person looks for Christians to make mistakes and then defines those Christians as hypocrites, then you will find them everywhere. Dr. Bob Chapman [7] stated in his book *Extreme Times for Extreme Lives* that if you want to follow Jesus Christ, it is all or nothing.

---

[7] Dr. Bob Chapman, Extreme times for extreme lives, living for Jesus in the 21st Century.

Notes

CHAPTER 2

Christianity and Religion

2.1 Why do Christians go through trials?

INTRODUCTION

I will endeavour to answer this question in two parts. The first part will be looking at the disciplinary aspect of God and the second will look at the altars erected against our lives to deprive us from prospering. One of the most difficult parts of the Christian life is the fact that becoming a disciple of Christ does not make us immune to life's trials and tribulations. As in all things, God's ultimate purpose for us is to grow more and more into the image of His Son (Romans 8:29). This is the goal of the Christian. Everything in life, including the trials and tribulations, is designed to enable us to reach that goal. It is part of the process of sanctification, being set apart for God's purposes and fitted to live for His glory.

Jesus Christ set the perfect example. "But God demonstrates His own love toward us, in that while we were yet sinners, Christ died for us" (Romans 5:8). These verses reveal aspects of His divine purpose for both Jesus Christ's trials and tribulations, as well as ours. Persevering proves our faith. "I can do all things through Christ, who strengthens me" (Philippians 4:13). The true believer's faith will be made sure by the trials we experience, so we can rest in the knowledge it is real and will last forever.

PART 1. SOME REASONS WHY CHRISTIANS HAVE TRIALS. IN MOST CASES GOD WANTS THE FOLLOWING TO HAPPEN

1. GLORIFY HIM (Daniel 3; 16 to 18, & 22-26)

16 Shadrach, Meshach and Abednego replied to him, "King Nebuchadnezzar, we do not need to defend ourselves before you in this matter. 17 If we are thrown into the blazing furnace, the God we serve is able to deliver us from it, and he will deliver us[b] from Your Majesty's hand. 18 But even if he does not, we want you to know, Your Majesty that we will not serve your gods or worship the image of gold you have set up. (Daniel 3:16-18, NIV)

> 22 The king's command was so urgent and the furnace so hot that the flames of the fire killed the soldiers who took up Shadrach, Meshach and Abednego, 23 and these three men, firmly tied, fell into the blazing furnace. 24 Then King Nebuchadnezzar leaped to his feet in amazement and asked his advisers, "Weren't there three men that we tied up and threw into the fire?" They replied, "Certainly, Your Majesty." 25 He said, "Look! I see four men walking around in the fire,

unbound and unharmed, and the fourth looks like a son of the gods." 26 Nebuchadnezzar then approached the opening of the blazing furnace and shouted, "Shadrach, Meshach and Abednego, servants of the Most High God, come out! Come here!" So Shadrach, Meshach and Abednego came out of the fire. (Daniel 3:22-26, NIV)

Trials develop godly character that enables us to "Rejoice in our sufferings, because we know that suffering produces perseverance; perseverance, character; and character, hope. And hope does not disappoint us, because God has poured out his love into our hearts by the Holy Spirit, whom he has given us" (Romans 5:3-5). The way trials accomplish this is explained in 1 Peter 1:6-7:

> In this you greatly rejoice, even though now for a little while, if necessary, you have been distressed by various trials, that the proof of your faith, being more precious than gold which perishes, even though tested by fire, may be found to result in praise and glory and honour at the revelation of Jesus Christ.

2. DISCIPLINING US FOR KNOWN SIN (Hebrews 12:4-1, NIV)

> In your struggle against sin, you have not yet resisted to the point of shedding your blood. 5 And have you completely forgotten this word of encouragement that addresses you as a father addresses his son? It says, "My son, do not make light of the Lord's discipline, and do not

lose heart when he rebukes you, 6 because the Lord disciplines the one he loves, and he chastens everyone he accepts as his son."7 Endure hardship as discipline; God is treating you as his children. For what children are not disciplined by their father? 8 If you are not disciplined—and everyone undergoes discipline—then you are not legitimate, not true sons and daughters at all. 9 Moreover, we have all had human fathers who disciplined us, and we respected them for it. How much more should we submit to the Father of spirits and live! 10 They disciplined us for a little while as they thought best; but God disciplines us for our good, in order that we may share in his holiness. 11 No discipline seems pleasant at the time, but painful. Later on, however, it produces a harvest of righteousness and peace for those who have been trained by it. (Read James 4:17, Romans 14:29 and 1 John 1:9) for more. (Hebrews 12:4-11, NIV)

It is never pleasant to be corrected and disciplined by God, but His discipline is a sign of deep love for us. When God corrects you, see it as proof of His love and ask Him what He is trying to teach you. Learn from that and obey His lead in your life. Do not lean on your own understanding and strength. Proverbs 16:1-9 tells us that God can do what no man can. It states:

> To humans belong the plans of the heart, but from the LORD comes the proper answer of the tongue. 2All a person's ways seem pure to

them, but motives are weighed by the LORD. 3Commit to the LORD whatever you do, and he will establish your plans. 4The LORD works out everything to its proper end- even the wicked for a day of disaster. 5The LORD detests all the proud of heart. Be sure of this: They will not go unpunished. 6Through love and faithfulness sin is atoned for; through the fear of the LORD evil is avoided. 7When the LORD takes pleasure in anyone's way, he causes their enemies to make peace with them. 8Better a little with righteousness than much gain with injustice. 9In their hearts humans plan their course, but the LORD establishes their steps.

3. PREVENT US FROM FALLING INTO SIN (1 Peter 4; 1-2, NIV)

Therefore, since Christ suffered in his body, arm yourselves also with the same attitude, because whoever suffers in the body is done with sin. 2 As a result, they do not live the rest of their earthly lives for evil human desires, but rather for the will of God. (1 Peter 4:1-2, NIV)

First, we have in verses 1 and 2 a general precept based upon the broad view of Christ's earthly history. "Christ hath suffered in the flesh." That is the great fact, which should shape the course of all His followers. But what does suffering in the flesh mean here? It does not refer only to the death of Jesus but to His entire life. The phrase "in the flesh" is reiterated in the context, and evidently, is equivalent to "during the earthly life." Our

Lord's life was, in one aspect, one continuous suffering because He lived the higher life of the Spirit.

4. KEEP US FROM PRIDE (2 Corinthians 12: 6 -10)

> Even if I should choose to boast, I would not be a fool, because I would be speaking the truth. But I refrain, so no one will think more of me than is warranted by what I do or say, or because of these surpassingly great revelations. Therefore, in order to keep me from becoming conceited or proud, I was given a thorn in my flesh, a messenger of Satan, to torment me. 8 Three times I pleaded with the Lord to take it away from me. 9 But he said to me, "My grace is sufficient for you, for my power is made perfect in weakness." Therefore, I will boast all the more gladly about my weaknesses, so that Christ's power may rest on me. 10 That is why, for Christ's sake, I delight in weaknesses, in insults, in hardships, in persecutions, in difficulties. For when I am weak, then I am strong. (2 Corinthians 12:6-10, NIV)

We don't know what Paul's thorn in the flesh was because he didn't tell us. But there were several suggestions that it could have been some kind of sickness or a disease (see Galatians 4: 13-14). The incident cannot be possibly identified with a recorded event in Paul's career, although there were also suggestions in Acts 14:19, 20. God refused to remove this thorn, which became a hindrance to Paul's ministry. Although God refused to remove the thorn, He continued to demonstrate His power on Paul and those around him. When we are strong in resources and abilities, we are tempted to take God's place and do His work on our own. That can lead to pride.

5. BUILD OUR FAITH (1 Peter 1:6-7)

> In this you greatly rejoice, even though now for a little while, if necessary, you have been distressed by various trials, that the proof of your faith, being more precious than gold which perishes, even though tested by fire, may be found to result in praise and glory and honour at the revelation of Jesus Christ. (1 Peter 1:6-7, NIV)

Why were Christians the target of persecution?

1. They refused to worship the emperor as a god and thus were viewed as atheists and traitors

2. They refused to worship in pagan temples so business for these moneymaking enterprises dropped whenever Christianity took hold

3. They didn't support the Roman ideals of self, power, and conquest and the Romans scorned the Christian ideal of self-sacrificing service

4. They exposed and rejected the horrible immorality of pagan culture

Finally, Peter mentioned suffering several times in this letter (1 Peter 1:6-7, 3:13-17, 4:12-19, 5:9). When he speaks of trials, he is not talking about natural disasters or the experience of God's punishments but the response of the unbelieving world to people of faith. All believers face such trials when they let their lights shine into the darkness. We must accept trials as part of the refining process that burns away impurities and prepares us to meet Christ.

6. CAUSE GROWTH (Romans 5:3-8)

> 3 Not only so, but we[a] also glory in our sufferings, because we know that suffering produces perseverance; 4 perseverance, character; and character, hope. 5 And hope does not put us to shame, because God's love has been poured out into our hearts through the Holy Spirit, who has been given to us. 6 You see, at just the right time, when we were still powerless, Christ died for the ungodly. 7 Very rarely will anyone die for a righteous person, though for a good person someone might possibly dare to die. 8 But God demonstrates his own love for us in this: While we were still sinners, Christ died for us. Not only so, but we also rejoice in our sufferings, because we know that suffering produces perseverance; perseverance, character; and character, hope. (Romans 5:3-8)

An Introduction to Some Unanswered Questions In Christendom

I love being around positive people perhaps because I am a "glass half full" kind of person. I love when people can see the positiveness in me even in the midst of situations that are distressful regardless of circumstances or obstacles. But the more I know people, the more I realize that this characteristic is a precious commodity. However, Paul reminds us, as Christians we can rejoice in the midst of any circumstance because of where our hope is placed. Hope is the highway that gets our faith from point A to point B. Hope is what keeps us moving and rejoicing through whatever circumstances life throws our way. So how do we have hope to see our faith realized?

We have hope when our faith is resting firmly in Jesus. Then it doesn't matter when suffering or persecution comes our way because hope lets us rejoice in the midst of it. James Chapter 1 says something similar, "Consider it pure joy, my brothers, whenever you face trials of many kinds, because you know that the testing of your faith develops perseverance" (James 1:2-3). Both Paul and James knew that a by-product of suffering at the hands of this world was perseverance. Patience is a fruit of the Spirit and necessary for Christians. Unlike the world's definition of patience, it is not a passive word but rather, a strong active word. The heart of patience denotes endurance, consistency, and perseverance no matter what happens.

Patience allows our faith to mature and produce hope. Hope gets us through to the end goal, which is the glory of God. As Christians, we should always be optimistic looking forward to Jesus' return for us. Jesus said, "In this world, you will have trouble, but take heart, I have overcome the world" (John 16:33). He knew the hope to which He was calling us. This blessed hope is what we await patiently for enduring and conquering in His name until His return. Praise God that this kind of hope does not disappoint!

7. TEACH OBEDIENCE AND CONTENTMENT (Acts 9:15-16)

> But the Lord said to Ananias, "Go! This man is my chosen instrument to proclaim my name to the Gentiles and their kings and to the people of Israel. 16. I will show him how much he must suffer for my name. NIV)

Faith in Christ brings great blessings but often come with great suffering too. Paul would suffer for his faith (2 Corinthians 11:23-27). God calls us to commitment not to comfort. But He promised to be with us through suffering and hardship, not to spare us from them. Saul was a chosen vessel to bear the gospel or to be the sower of seed (Psalm 126:6) "before the Gentiles," or nations of the world. He was an apostle and teacher of the Gentiles in faith and verity. The gospel of the uncircumcision was particularly committed to him: and before "kings", as he did before

Agrippa, king of the Jews, and before Nero, emperor of Rome; and his bonds for the Gospel, and so the Gospel through his bonds became manifest in all the palace, or court of Caesar. And before the children of Israel;

Even though Saul was heading to Damascus to capture the believers, Ananias found him as the Lord instructed and greeted him as "Brother Saul." Ananias feared this meeting because of Saul's intention. Nevertheless, he showed him love. We know it's hard to show love to someone who is about to make us prisoners for our faith.

> I am not saying this because I am in need, for I have learned to be content whatever the circumstances. 12. I know what it is to be in need, and I know what it is to have plenty. I have learned the secret of being content in any and every situation, whether well fed or hungry, whether living in plenty or in want. 13. I can do all this through him who gives me strength. (Philippians 4:11-13, NIV)

Contentment can be an elusive pursuit. We go after what we think will make us happy only to find that it didn't work. In fact, we were happier before we started the quest. It's like the story of two teardrops floating down the river of life. One teardrop said to the other, "Who are you?" "I'm a teardrop from a girl who loved a man and lost him. "Who are you?" The other asked" "I'm a teardrop from the girl who got him." Ha! Ha! Ha! Ha!

Funny, isn't it? But not really, what you don't treasure, others do. What you neglect, others look after. Life is a vicious cycle. It is also not getting what you are looking for that will bring happiness to you.

8. EQUIP US TO COMFORT OTHERS (2 Corinthians 1:3-4)

> Praise be to the God and Father of our Lord Jesus Christ, the Father of compassion and the God of all comfort, 4 who comforts us in all our troubles, so that we can comfort those in any trouble with the comfort we ourselves receive from God. (2 Corinthians 1:3-4, NIV)

Many think that when God comforts us, our troubles will go away. But if that were the case, we would only turn to God out of our desire to be relieved of pain, not out of love for Him. We must understand that being "comforted" can also mean receiving strength, encouragement, and hope to deal with our troubles. The more we suffer the more comfort we receive from God. If you are feeling overwhelmed, allow God to comfort you. Remember that every trial you endure will help you and other people who are suffering from similar troubles.

After going through deceit, disappointments, betrayals, and resentment, I finally found peace when God called me to ministry. My ministry is to discern, evangelise, deliver, baptise, and assist believers on their journey to seeking God and becoming disciples of Jesus.

9. PROVIDE THE REALITY OF CHRIST IN US (2 Corinthians 4:7-11)

> But we have this treasure in jars of clay to show that this all-surpassing power is from God and not from us. We are hard pressed on every side, but not crushed; perplexed, but not in despair; persecuted, but not abandoned; struck down, but not destroyed. We always carry around in our body the death of Jesus, so that the life of Jesus may also be revealed in our body. For we who are alive are always being given over to death for Jesus' sake, so that his life may also be revealed in our mortal body. (2 Corinthians 4:7-11, NIV)

The supremely valuable message of salvation in Jesus Christ has been entrusted by God to frail and fallible human beings. Paul's focus, however, was not on the perishable container but on its priceless contents. God uses us to spread His good news, and He gives us power to do His work. Knowing that the power is God's, not ours, should keep us from pride and motivate us to keep daily contact with God, our power source. Our responsibility is to let people see God through us. This can only happen if we are totally available and radically obedient.

10. GIVE TESTIMONIES TO ANGELS (Ephesians 3:8-11)

> Although I am less than the least of all the Lord's people, this grace was given me: to preach to the Gentiles the boundless riches of

Christ, 9 and to make plain to everyone the administration of this mystery, which for ages past was kept hidden in God, who created all things. 10 His intent was that now, through the church, the manifold wisdom of God should be made known to the rulers and authorities in the heavenly realms, 11 according to his eternal purpose that he accomplished in Christ Jesus our Lord. 12 In him and through faith in him we may approach God with freedom and confidence. 13 I ask you, therefore, not to be discouraged because of my sufferings for you, which are your glory. (Ephesians 3:8-11, NIV)

When Paul describes himself as "the least deserving Christian there is," he means that he cannot do his work without the help of God. Yet, God chose him to share the good news with the Gentiles and gave him the power to do so. In most cases, if we feel inadequate in our roles, we must not forget the difference God makes in equipping us with the necessary powers to do his work. "How does God want to use you? Draw on his power, do your part, and faithfully perform the special role God has called you to play in his plan. It is an awesome privilege to be able to approach God with freedom and confidence" (Dr. Natanael Costea, *Forty Years and Forty Days* book). Dr. Costea's book is worth reading.

2.2. If the God we are following is that powerful, why does He allow evil or bad things to happen to good people?

After the answers given above about Christians having trials, one will wonder why God would permit bad things to happen to good people. Because of my understanding of what the Bible says, I will begin by saying yes, God allows "bad" things to happen, but God does not cause them. As humans, God gave us freedom to do whatever we are pleased to do but through that freedom, we open portals that encourage the Devil to enter our lives. We are spirits with souls that live in bodies, which are the flesh. If we allow our flesh to be corrupted, then we suffer the consequences.

The Bible tells us in Galatians 5:13-14, "You, my brothers and sisters, were called to be free. But do not use your freedom to indulge the flesh; rather, serve one another humbly in love. 14 For the entire law is fulfilled in keeping this one command: 'Love your neighbour as yourself.'"

The book of Job deals with the issue of why God allows bad things to happen to good people. As we all read in the Bible, Job was a righteous man (Job 1:1); yet, he suffered in ways that are almost beyond belief. God permitted Satan to do everything he wanted to Job, but he warned him not to kill him. Satan did his vilest. What was Job's reaction to all of this? "Though he slayed me, yet will I hope in him" (Job 13:15). "The LORD gave, and the LORD has taken away; may the name of the LORD be praised" (Job 1:21). Job did not understand why God had allowed the things He did, but he knew God was good; therefore, he continued to trust in Him. Ultimately, that should be our reaction as well.

Why do evil things happen to good people? As hard as it is to acknowledge, we must remember that there are no "good" people, in the absolute sense of the word. All of us are tainted by and infected with sin. To corroborate this statement, I invite you to read Ecclesiastes 7:20, Romans 3:23, and 1 John 1:8. As Jesus said, "No one is good except God alone" (Luke 18:19). All of us feel the effects of sin in one way or another. Sometimes it's our personal sins; other times, it's the sins of others. The world we live in is fallen because of sin, and we are currently experiencing that fall. Examples of the effects of the fall are unfairness and meaningless suffering. When wondering why God would allow bad things to happen to people, it's also good to consider the reasons why these things happen in the first place.

The apostle Paul was very quick to state clearly that this world is not the end so when bad things happen, Christians should know they have an eternal standpoint as stated in 2 Corinthians 4:16–18, "We do not lose heart. Though outwardly we are wasting away, yet inwardly we are being renewed day by day. For our light and momentary troubles are achieving for us an eternal glory that far outweighs them all. So, we fix our eyes not on what is seen, but on what is unseen, since what is seen is temporary, but what is unseen is eternal." This means that we will have a reward someday, and it will be glorious.

Secondly, bad things may happen to good people because God uses those bad things for an ultimate, lasting good. Romans 8:28, says, "We know that in all things God works for the good of those who love him, who have been called according to his purpose." Joseph's brothers thought they had gotten rid of him by selling him as a slave. However, God knew His plans for him. Even though he went through his horrific sufferings, He finally saw God's good plan in it all (Genesis 50:19–21).

Thirdly, bad things happen to good people because through those bad things, they are equipped as strong believers for deeper ministry. Paul mentioned this in 2 Corinthians 1:3-5:

> Praise be to the Father of compassion and the God of all comfort, who comforts us in all our troubles, so that we can comfort those in any trouble with the comfort we ourselves receive from God. For just as we share abundantly in the sufferings of Christ, so also our comfort abounds through Christ.

People with battle scars can better help others going through battles. All we need is support from fellow intercessors.

Fourthly, bad things happen to good people and the worst things happen to the best of people. Jesus was the only truly Righteous One. Yet, He suffered more than we can imagine. If we want to follow His footsteps, we must be ready to suffer all kinds of attacks and endure it.

> If suffer for doing good and you endure it, this is commendable before God. To this you were called, because Christ suffered for you, leaving you an example, that you should follow in his steps. 'He committed no sin, and no deceit was found in his mouth.' When they hurled their insults at him, he did not retaliate; when he suffered, he made no threats. Instead, he entrusted himself to him who judges justly. (1 Peter 2:20-23)

Jesus is no stranger to our pain.

> Dear friends, do not be surprised at the fiery ordeal that has come on you to test you, as though something strange were happening to you. 13"But rejoice inasmuch as you participate in the sufferings of Christ, so that you may be overjoyed when his glory is revealed. 14 If you are insulted because of the name of Christ, you are blessed, for the Spirit of glory and of God rests on you. 15 If you suffer, it should not be as a murderer or thief or any other kind of criminal, or even as a meddler. 16 However, if you suffer as a Christian, do not be ashamed, but praise God that you bear that name. 17 For it is time for judgment to begin with God's household; and if it begins with us, what will the outcome be for those who do not obey the gospel of God? 18 And, "If it is hard for the righteous to be saved, what will

become of the ungodly and the sinner?" 19 So then, those who suffer according to God's will should commit themselves to their faithful Creator and continue to do good. (1 Peter 4:12-19)

"But God demonstrates his own love for us in this: While we were still sinners, Christ died for us" (Romans 5:8). Despite the sinful nature of the people of this world, God still loves us. Jesus loved us enough to die to take the penalty for our sins (Romans 6:23). If we receive Jesus Christ as Saviour (John 3:16; Romans 10:9), we will be forgiven and promised an eternal home in heaven (Romans 8:1).

God allows things to happen for a reason. Whether or not we understand His reasons, we must remember that God is good, just, loving, and merciful (Psalm 135:3). Often, bad things happen to us that we simply cannot understand. Instead of doubting God's goodness, our reaction should be to trust Him. "Trust in the LORD with all your heart and lean not on your own understanding; in all your ways acknowledge Him, and He will make your paths straight" (Proverbs 3:5–6).

We walk by faith, not by sight. If by any chance you are going through some unexplained difficulties, sickness, disease, hard times at work or nothing seems to work in your life, the chances are, you need deliverance from witchcraft altars or generational curses. This could also be a reason for the bad things that are happening to your life. The following are but a few signs that evil altars are erected against you or your ministry. The followings signs are also evidence that the spirits from those altars are the ones responsible for maintaining such evil patterns.

- Are you hated by others for no reason? Then the chances are you are under bondage.
- Is there a feeling of cobwebs on your body when there is no visible sign of them?
- Are you experiencing sleep paralysis after visiting the doctor on several occasions?
- Do you feel your bed shaking or vibrating sometimes or all the time? This is an indication that some spirits that are not of God are after your life.
- Do you smell or feel the presence of strange odours all the time on your body or your home? This indicates the existence of the spirit of infirmity waiting to strike. You need deliverance.
- Are you eating or being fed in your dreams? That's poisoning and you need deliverance.
- Do you keep dreaming about snakes? This means that the Enemy is on your case. He is trying to instil fear to make you constantly frustrated and confused. This may eventually lead to major bouts of depression.
- Are you overwhelmingly jealous and have a bad temper or anger? Those are spirits that cause retrogression because they always make you think negatively.

- Do you physically feel things moving or crawling on your body when nothing is there? You visit the doctor and he/she finds nothing. Look for a Bible-based church and give or rededicate your life to Christ. Get deliverance and be set free. There is nothing impossible with God.
- Are you experiencing defilement by having sex in a dream that makes you lose all desire for your partner or spouse? This is caused by illegal underworld spirit men or women who come to defile you. That must be broken.
- Are you experiencing a moment where everyone wants to sleep with you but do not want to marry you? Or do you want to only sleep with women you don't want to marry? This is the spirit of Jezebel and Ahab. It must be broken.
- There are people who are only attracted to married men or women. This could be a generational curse that must have been passed from one generation to the other. As a biomedical scientist myself, we call that epigenetics. Epigenetics is the study of heritable phenotype changes that do not involve alterations in the DNA sequence. The Greek prefix "epi" in epigenetics implies features that are "on top of" or "in addition to" the traditional genetic basis for inheritance. Epigenetics most often denotes changes that affect gene activity and expression but can also be used to describe any heritable phenotypic changes.
- Are you experiencing failure at the edge of success?

- Is there anything your family has gone through that you are currently experiencing?
- Are you experiencing instability in your marriage, relationships or having difficulty conceiving?
- Are you constantly dreaming of your dead parents or relatives? It's a spirit of death hovering over you. And the list goes on.
- Is your ministry or church in tremendous debt, living above their means, and putting a burden on the membership to pay these debts?
- Are there ministry leaders who dismiss the fact that witchcraft, obeah, voodoo, etc. exists?
- Is your church or ministry a nest for attracting false prophets? In this case, members are not valued.
- Are ministry leaders in the habit of exhibiting behaviours that constantly make them announce that they are the leaders and this is their church? Exhibiting manipulative and controlling spirits is tantamount to witchcraft.

If you are experiencing any of the above, the chances are a series of altars have been erected against your progress and life. But guess what? Jesus paid it all. It is only him we owe. His blood became the price that cleansed us from all this nonsense. If you observe any of the above signs, do not pray for the people. Instead, pray against the evil altars controlling them. Make no mistake, if you have practiced any form of witchcraft whether you did it to buy luck, harm someone or remove a curse from yourself, for certain, the very altar you consulted to achieve your objectives is the very altar working against you! The ultimate purpose of an evil altar is to hijack the God-intended destiny of the victim and replace it with a destiny of hardship and oppression from Satan. Bottom line, destinies are exchanged at evil altars!

2.3 Religion: When a Muslim criticizes Jesus, it's no offence but when a Christian does criticize Mohamed or Islam, it becomes a world issue. Why?

To answer this question, may I first of all thank a Christian brother by the name of Mark Moinjeh who posted the following, and requested an answer from my quest to address some issues that are of major concern to other Christians. This is what Mark said on the 7th of January 2017,

> As a Christian and a former Muslim, what I have found difficult to understand in Christendom and difficult to also describe is and you will agree with me on that is:

- Christianity existed before Islam
- Christianity was in every part of the middle east as a major religion
- The spread of Christianity in those parts was peaceful; as a result, it was very accommodating
- It didn't prevent the existence of other faiths or wage war on them either

- The Christians have always been law abiding people. And you will also agree with me that
- Islam was the next religion founded after Christianity and Judaism
- It was spread by jehad they call holy war
- Christians were subjected to forced conversion
- Their lands were taken when they were conquered as it happened recently in Syria when ISIS forced the Christians to convert to Islam, be killed or leave their land. Their women were taken as sex slaves trading in them
- Churches were burnt and some desecrated

With just these few points mentioned above, Christianity being the first religion after Judaism and before Islam was practiced almost in every part of the world. What is the entire Christian body doing to stop the aggression against Christians in the Middle East and in other parts of the world? Is it because we are divided along denominational lines that we cannot speak with one voice as a fulfillment of the scripture of a divided house against itself cannot stand?

On the contrary, you will see that when Muslims are affected in a non-dominated Muslim country for political or religious reasons, you will see Muslims almost all over the world protesting, and in response, the world will condemn it but when it happens to Christians, it is not important. For example, recently in Indonesia as the case is ongoing, a Christian governor is being persecuted for blasphemy. His persecutors are asking for his removal and that he is jailed because he is a Christian, and a Christian cannot rule majority Muslims according to them, but a Muslim can be a mayor in majority Christian city in London. Christianity/church is forbidden in Saudi Arabia, but mosques are allowed in the Vatican and everywhere in the Christendom.

Today, biblical facts are being claimed by the Islamic religion with the world supporting them and against Christians preserving their heritage. How can Israel or Palestine be more important to the Muslims than the Jews and the Christians, but the world is against the Christians and the Jews preserving those facts as their heritage. In all these happenings, where are the Christians to defend their brothers and sisters being persecuted, sexually abused, enslaved, their heritages destroyed, they are driven from their homes, they are forced to bow down to idols and the world is silent about them. This is what I do not understand about the Christendom. Thank you my brother. Your brother Mark.

Wow! This brother made me to think twice before answering these series of questions and vital points he made in his correspondence to me. The points he made were a mouthful and contain a lot of wisdom, but they are encompassed with frustration. To assist me in responding to him, I also sought the wisdom of Dr. Nathanael Costea, the principal of the Australian School of Ministry (ASOM). This was Dr. Costea's response on the 8 January 2017:

> Hi Francis, I hear his deep concern and cry of the heart, and Mark has a point. I do believe there are many Christians doing amazing works strategically behind the scenes. Recent times have also taught us that we do have a voice, a much stronger voice than we realize (i.e. defending marriage in Australia, Donald Trump winning the US elections, etc.). My personal concern is that we seem to be mainly on the defensive rather than on the offensive. Somehow though, Christ sees us through - and that's where my peace comes from. God is still fighting for us and will do until the end. We are responsible though and should do more. In God's abundant goodness,
>
> Pastor Natanael Costea.

As a former Muslim myself, I found this very interesting because God Himself was very clear to Mohammed in the book of Surah Aal Imran Chapter 3 verses 15 to 23. It states:

> Say, "Shall I inform you of [something] better than that? For those who fear God will be gardens in the presence of their Lord beneath which rivers flow, wherein they abide eternally, and purified spouses and approval from God. And in Him is Seeing of His servants. vs16

Those who say, "Our Lord, indeed we have believed, so forgive us our sins and protect us from the punishment of the Fire, v17 says "The patient, the true, the obedient, those who spend their time with God and those who seek forgiveness before dawn. Vs18" God witnesses that there is no deity except Him, and so do the angels and those of knowledge - that He is maintaining creation in justice. There is no deity except Him, the Exalted in Might, the Wise. Vs 19 says Indeed, the religion in the sight of Allah is the one that preaches the Gospel of Jesus **(Note; here that the Arabs have removed Christianity and replaced it with Islam).** And those who were given the Scripture did not differ except after knowledge had come to them - out of jealous animosity between themselves. And whoever disbelieves in the verses of God, then indeed, He is swift in taking account. **Vs20 is the further controversial verse where God gave Mohammad the following instructions** "So if they argue with you, say, "I have submitted myself to God and so have those who follow me." And say to those who were given the Scripture before you and to the unlearned, "Have you submitted yourselves to the Lord?" And if they submit, they are rightly guided; but if they turn away - then upon you is only the duty of notification. And God is Seeing of His servants. Vs21 Those who disbelieve in the signs of God and kill the prophets without right and kill those who order justice from among the people - give them tidings of a painful punishment. Vs22 They are the ones whose deeds have become worthless in this world and the Hereafter, and for them there will be no helpers. Vs 23" Do you not consider, O Muhammad, those who were given a portion of the Scripture? They are invited to the Scripture of Allah that it should arbitrate between them; then a party of them turns away, and they are refusing the truth.[8]

Well, fellow believers, those Muslims who persecute Christians for the sake of Mohammed will face punishment because the Bible tells us that the battle is not ours. "And he said, 'Listen, all Judah and inhabitants of Jerusalem and King Jehoshaphat: Thus says the Lord to you,' Do not be afraid and do not be dismayed at this great horde, for the battle is not yours but God's" (2 Chronicles 20:15). Fanatic Muslims who fight a physical fight to defend their God or Mohammed do not read the Quran. To prove to you more facts, verse 3 of Chapter 3 of Surah Aal Imran says this: "He has sent down upon you, O Muhammad, the Book of truth, confirming

---

[8] Imran in Islam is regarded as the father of Mary (mother of Jesus). This chapter is named after the family of Imran, which includes Imran, Saint Anne, Mary, and Jesus. Regarding the timing and contextual background of the supposed revelation (Asbāb al-nuzūl), the chapter is believed to have been either the second or third of the Medinan surahs, as it references both the events of Badr and the Uhud. Almost all of it also belongs to the third year of the Hijra, though a minority of its verses might have been revealed during the visit of the Najrān Christian deputation and the Mubahala, which occurred around the 10th year of the Hijrah.[2] This chapter primarily focuses on the departure of prophethood from the Mosaic dispensation. (Dawood, N J (31 October 2019). The Koran. London: Penguin Books. p. 306.)

what was before you. And He revealed the Torah and the Gospel." A true Muslim who wants salvation will give his life to Christ and be saved.

Remember that the weapons we fight with are not of this world. "The weapons we fight with are not the weapons of the world. On the contrary, they have divine power to demolish strongholds. We demolish arguments and every pretension that sets itself up against the knowledge of God, and we take captive every thought and make it obedient to Christ" (2 Corinthians 10:4–5, NIV). See also 2 Kings 20:1-7, which is a typical example to show you how God can fight for us.

In Romans 12:9-21, the Bible says we should hate what is evil and hold on to what is good. Also, we should keep the spiritual fervor, serve the Lord and be patient in afflictions. It also says we should not pay evil for evil. God says vengeance is His. He will repay. This can only happen if our hearts are in tune with God's heart. Dr. Costea stated in Chapter 36 of his book *Forty Years and Forty Days* that "God wants our hearts to be in tune with His heart for He is a God of the heart. He scrutinizes the heart of everyone for that is where He wants to reside. Only a seeker with a true heart will find God and only those who find God find true love." So let us show our persecutors love as stated in 1 Corinthians 13:1-8.

Notes

CHAPTER 3

The Ministry of Jesus vs. the Ministry of Men

Before talking about the ministry of Jesus Christ, I want to throw light on who this man was and His purpose for coming to this world. I will also examine the blueprints of His deity and His preparation for ministry.

> In the beginning [before all-time] was the Word ([a]Christ), and the Word was with God, and [b]the Word was God Himself. 2 He was [continually existing] in the beginning [co-eternally] with God. Verses 12-14 says "Yet to all who did receive him, to those who believed in his name, he gave the right to become children of God 13 children born not of natural descent, nor of human decision or a husband's will, but born of God. 14 The Word became flesh and made his dwelling among us. We have seen his glory, the glory of the one and only Son, who came from the Father, full of grace and truth. (John 1:1-2, 12 &14)

John makes it very clear that Jesus is not a man. He is the eternal Son of God. He is the light of the world because He offers the gift of eternal life to all mankind. How foolish and blind we would be not to recognize His deity. If Jesus is the eternal Son of God, we should pay attention to His divine identity and His life-giving message.

In preparing for His ministry, Jesus met with individuals, preachers, and teachers of the law. He attracted great crowds of people who came to listen to His teachings. But that did not stop there. Jesus trained His disciples for the challenge ahead of them. Jesus also debated with religious leaders but when some of them heard that He was the Son of God, they had mixed reactions. However, those who believed worshipped Him.

My beloved, we see the same reactions today because times have changed, and most people have hardened their hearts against even listening to the gospel let alone telling about the kingdom of God. Jesus carefully instructed His disciples how to continue His legacy after He had gone to His Father. Jesus taught His disciples that the Holy Spirit would come after He ascended into heaven from the earth. The Holy Spirit will then dwell amongst them, guide, counsel, and comfort those who follow His teaching and ministry.

In John 1:15-17, we see how John pointed out to the crowd about who Jesus Christ is and His purpose. In the synoptic gospels, the ministry of Jesus began with His baptism in the countryside of Roman Judea and Transjordan, near the River Jordan and ends in Jerusalem following the

Last Supper with His disciples. The Gospel of Luke (3:23) states that Jesus was "about 30 years of age" when He started His ministry. A sequence of events of Jesus typically has the date of the start of His ministry estimated at around AD 27–29 and the end between AD 30–36.

3.1 If the body of Christ is one, why are there so many churches doing different things in the name of Jesus?

To answer this question, I endeavored to look at 2 Peter 2: 1-10 which says:

> But there were also false prophets among the people, just as there will be false teachers among you. They will secretly introduce destructive heresies, even denying the sovereign LORD who bought them-bringing swift destruction on themselves. 2Many will follow their depraved conduct and will bring the way of truth into disrepute. 3In their greed these teachers will exploit you with fabricated stories. Their condemnation has long been hanging over them, and their destruction has not been sleeping. 4For if God did not spare angels when they sinned, but sent them to hell, putting them in chains of darkness to be held for judgment; 5if he did not spare the ancient world when he brought the flood on its ungodly people, but protected Noah, a preacher of righteousness, and seven others; 6if he condemned the cities of Sodom and Gomorrah by burning them to ashes, and made them an example of what is going to happen to the

ungodly; 7and if he rescued Lot, a righteous man, who was distressed by the depraved conduct of the lawless 8(for that righteous man, living among them day after day, was tormented in his righteous soul by the lawless deeds he saw and heard)- 9if this is so, then the LORD knows how to rescue the godly from trials and to hold the unrighteous for punishment on the day of judgment. 10This is especially true of those who follow the corrupt desire of the flesh and despise authority. Bold and arrogant, they are not afraid to heap abuse on celestial beings.

As we currently live in a world of political correctness, I believe all people can do what they think is right for them in the name of our Lord and Saviour Jesus Christ. The New Living Translation Bible stated what apostle Paul was trying to sink in the minds of the people of Corinth in his first letter. "You say, 'I am allowed to do anything'--but not everything is good for you. You say, 'I am allowed to do anything'--but not everything is beneficial" (1 Corinthians 10:23). So most of these churches opened in the name of worship are cartels of spiritual mind control and manipulative altars. They preach prosperity and miracle money messages because people are desperate for quick answers to their problems.

When people who know what is right or wrong come to worship in such places, these cartel leaders will influence the congregation they have succeeded in manipulating to castigate the true worshippers. I am saying this because I became a victim of circumstances after being invited to a similar cartel. God gave my wife and me the spirit of discernment to pick up what was going on in such a cartel. The head of that ministry was full of pride. He did not want to talk to anyone or answer questions with regards to the subjective and manipulative tendencies in that church of six (6) people. So, in such cases, only the prayers of faithful servants will shut the doors of places of that nature.

Here is a message I preached on respecting pastors and elders and what I thought was wrong with most churches and believers today. This will also be found in Chapter 4 of this book.

Pastors and church leaders or elders are expected to be qualified as stated in 1Timothy 3:1-10.

Qualifications for Overseers and Deacons

> Here is a trustworthy saying: Whoever aspires to be an overseer desires a noble task. 2 Now the overseer is to be above reproach, faithful to his wife, temperate, self-controlled, respectable, hospitable, able to teach, 3 not given to drunkenness, not violent but gentle, not quarrelsome, not a lover of money. 4 He must manage his own family well and see that his children obey him, and he must do so in a manner worthy of full[a] respect. 5 (If anyone does not know how to manage his own family, how can he take care of God's church?) 6 He must not be a recent convert, or he may become

conceited and fall under the same judgment as the devil. 7 He must also have a good reputation with outsiders, so that he will not fall into disgrace and into the devil's trap. 8 In the same way, deacons[b] are to be worthy of respect, sincere, not indulging in much wine, and not pursuing dishonest gain. 9 They must keep hold of the deep truths of the faith with a clear conscience. 10 They must first be tested; and then if there is nothing against them, let them serve as deacons.

We all know what Paul was saying to Timothy: pastors and church elders must be respected and honoured but not worshipped. Most African believers today have been caught up in the trap of worshipping their pastors or prophets more than their God and their husbands. If you are one of those people who bow down to humans, I am referring to you now. Stop It! These men of God are humans like you and they have not died on the cross for you. Their blood did not pay the price for your salvation. Read your Bibles very carefully. I tend to blame some of you who are making these men and women of God pompous. Some of them had humble beginnings but as time went on, self-glory, self-pride and the hunger for fame cropped in. They were then immersed in the lust of the flesh as stated in 1 John 2:16: "For everything in the world—the lust of the flesh, the lust of the eyes, and the pride of life—comes not from the Father but from the world" (NIV).

The next thing we see coming is that the congregation is subjected to financial stress, duress, and anxiety. These are the things that lead to mental illness, which is a curse and demonic suppression. The Bible is the Word of God that is clear cut on such oppressive behaviours. Read it for free!

> Cursed is the one who trusts in man, who draws strength from mere flesh and whose heart turns away from the Lord. 6 That person will be like a bush in the wastelands; they will not see prosperity when it comes. They will dwell in the parched places of the desert, in a salt land where no one lives. (Jeremiah 17:5-8, NIV)

Stop putting their photos and accessories on your cars and walls in your houses. It's demonic. Put your confidence in the Lord only.

No wonder why some of you are sick and can't find a cure for an infirmity you are suffering from. Open your eyes and see how they are becoming rich through your stupidity. The Holy Spirit is gentle and kind. He does not subject people to mental torture, psychological oppression, and depression. Wherever the Spirit of the Lord is there is freedom. Some of these pastors and prophets have been given a second chance to repent, but they won't. This is what the Bible tells us God will do to them as you have read from 2 Peter 2:1-10.

3.2 Does it feel like churches are empty and the spiritual paddocks are bare?

The answer to this question is yes. Well, one will further ask why. One of the facilitators of the Australian Prayer Network, Matthew Bolte once gave us a picture of what a mega church with many benches and few people look like. See below:

No sheep in the yards

(Photograph, Thanks to The Australian Prayer Network)

We Have a History of Praying for Revival

Many churches today have been caught up in compromising the gospel of Jesus. They preach the gospel of men. Church budgets and giving are preached about more than the gospel of Jesus in today's churches. Gossip, slander, and offence have been planted in churches causing people to run away from the house of God. If we want our churches to have worshippers again, we need a Spirit of grace, a spirit of supplication, deep conviction of sin, and a fountain to be opened. God will answer our pleas.

> And I will pour out on the house of David and the inhabitants of Jerusalem a spirit of grace and supplication. They will look on me, the one they have pierced, and they will mourn for him as one mourns for an only child, and grieve bitterly for him as one grieves for a firstborn son. (Zechariah 12:10)

God can easily forgive our church leaders who mess with His kingdom business. If we pray with sincerity, His mercies can come upon us. But how should we pray? We should pray with visible unity, explicit agreement and urgent, extraordinary prayers pleading for the Holy Spirit whom we have grieved in one way or the other. "And the inhabitants of one city will go to another and say, 'Let us go at once to entreat the LORD and seek the LORD Almighty. I myself am going" (Zechariah 8:21).

In one of his teachings, Matthew Bolte said, "Pray when the yards are empty, and the paddocks are dry." Does it feel as if the churches of Australia and around the world are empty and the spiritual paddocks of these nations are bare? Can we cry out with Isaiah, "I have laboured to no purpose; I have spent my strength in vain and for nothing" (Isaiah 49:4)? Is your soul thirsty for more of God but wherever you turn it just feels like more of the same? Are you longing for God to "rend the heavens and come down" (Isaiah 64:1)? When King David felt pressed in on every side and his soul was thirsty, when he felt spiritually unsatisfied he set his mind to what God had done in the past and that gave him hope. "I remember the days of long ago, I meditate on all your works

And consider what your hands have done (Psalm 143:5).

Perhaps it is time to turn our minds to what God has done in the past in these nations. He has done great things in this nation but many of us from this generation have not been told the praiseworthy deeds of the Lord (cf Psalm 78:4). As we see what He has done and read our very own history of the mighty outpourings of God's Spirit, let faith arise. Let the faith that believes if it has happened in these nations before it can happen again come forth. We must have faith to believe that God not only wants to pour out His Spirit in this nation but that it is His will and purpose to do so. And if it is His will, then it would behoove us to pray according to His will.

Jonathon Edwards [9] puts it this way:

---

[9] Thomas A. Schafer (1988) wrote the history of Jonathon Edwards; on Praying together for revival pp55 -59. Jonathan Edwards was an American revivalist preacher, philosopher, and Congregationalist Protestant theologian. Edwards is widely regarded as one of America's most important and original philosophical theologians.

> The sum of the blessings Christ sought, by what He did and suffered in the work of redemption was the Holy Spirit. The Holy Spirit, in His indwelling, His influences and fruits, is the sum of all grace, holiness, comfort and joy, or in one word, of all the spiritual good Christ purchased for men in this world; and is the sum of all perfection, glory and eternal joy, that He purchased for them in another world. (*Praying Together for Revival*, pp55)

He then draws this stunning conclusion about the focus of our prayer:

> If ... this is what Jesus Christ, our great Redeemer and the head of the church, did so much desire, and set His heart upon, from all eternity, and which He died and suffered so much for, offering up "strong crying and tears" (Hebrews 5:7), and His precious blood to obtain it; surely His disciples and members should also earnestly seek it, and be much and earnest in prayer for it. (*Praying Together for Revival*, pp59)

So if we desire to see "all the spiritual good Christ purchased for all men" made freely available in these nations then perhaps we need to be in "much and earnest prayer." But how do we pray? How can we pray if we don't know what to pray for? How can we pray if we have no faith to believe that it could happen in these nations? (Schafer, Thomas A. 1988).

Here is an extract from a book written by Jonathon Edwards, Northampton shire, England 1784 and The Prayer Call, [10]

> By the mid 1780's the Baptist Church in England was in serious decline. In the spring of 1784 an English Baptist pastor, Rev John Sutcliff of Olney, was handed a copy of Jonathon Edwards book "A Humble Attempt", it had a profound impact on Sutcliff. That June, at the annual meeting of the Northampton shire Baptist Association, he proposed that the churches of the association establish monthly prayer meetings for the outpouring of God's Holy Spirit. This proposal was a call for them "to wrestle with God for the effusion of His Holy Spirit.

This English preacher, after recommending that there should be corporate prayers for one hour on the first Monday evening of the month, the call, most likely drawn up by Sutcliff, continued:

> The grand object in prayer is to be, that the Holy Spirit may be poured down on our ministers and churches, that sinners may be converted, the saints edified, the interest of religion revived, and the name of God glorified. At the same time remember, we trust you will not confine your requests to your own societies (i.e. churches) or to your own immediate connection (i.e. denomination); let the whole interest of Redeemer be affectionately remembered, and the spread of the

---

[10] Jonathon Edwards "A Humble Attempt", England 1784 and The Prayer Call

gospel to the most distant parts of the habitable globe be the object of your most fervent requests. We shall rejoice if any other Christian societies of our own or other denomination will unite with us and do now invite them most cordially to join heart and hand in the attempt. (The 18th Century Great Commission Resurgence; Part 2. Praying for Revival. by Michael Haykin.pp1)

So, we need ministers of like mindedness to call for prayers if we want to see a revival and the paddock replenished). [11]

On this note, I feel that likeminded ministers should come together and constantly pray for the nations they live in or belong to so that revival and replenishment of the paddock can occur. Jesus said: "My sheep know my voice."

---

[11] (The 18th Century Great Commission Resurgence; Part 2. Praying for revival. by Michael Haykin pp 1)

Notes

CHAPTER 4

How Do We Honour And Respect Our Elders, Including Our Pastors?

There are many ways to respect and honour your elders and your pastors. But let us start with your elders. Young men and women ought to:

- **Give elderly people your time and assistance.** Visit them in their homes. If they are already in nursing homes, go there and show them love; assist them with some chores. "The glory of young men is their strength, but the splendour of old men is their gray hair" (Proverbs 20:29).
- **Talk to elderly people with respect.** Use manners when speaking to them. Don't talk to them how you would talk to your friends. These people have done a lot in life, even if you think they haven't. "Do not speak harshly to an older man but encourage him as you would a father, younger men as brothers, older women as mothers, younger women as sisters, in all purity" (1 Timothy 5:1-2).

- **Listen to them whilst they are talking; you may miss something by interrupting.** Listen to the stories about their lives. Grasp something of significance from them.

Listen to advice and accept instruction, that you may gain wisdom in the future. (Proverbs 19:20)

You shall stand up before the grey head and honor the face of an old man, and you shall fear your God: I am the Lord. (Leviticus 19:32)

Children, obey your parents in the Lord, for this is right. (Ephesians 6:1)

- **Finally, be patient with them and be a friend.** Aging is a process; you will be there tomorrow.

Honour your father and mother,' and 'love your neighbour as yourself. (Matthew 19:19) Whoever is patient has great understanding, but one who is quick-tempered displays folly. (Proverbs 14:29).

As I mentioned in Chapter 3, pastors and church leaders or elders are expected to be qualified as stated in 1Timothy 3:1-10 (Qualifications for Overseers and Deacons).

Churches must not be in a haste to appoint an elder or ordain a pastor whose character in the church is questionable. As mentioned in the previous chapters, most African believers today have been caught in the trap of worshipping their pastors or prophets more than their God. Some women respect their pastors more than they respect their own husbands. Believers should try to change their mindsets. These men of God are humans like you. Respect them but don't worship them. It is a thin line and a big difference between serving God and man. Put your confidence in the Lord only. Mark Dance of Lifeway Leadership ministry says:

1. WE SHOULD HONOUR OUR PASTORS BY SUPPORTING THEM

Yes, I totally agree objectively because no shepherd should force his sheep to support him. They should do so willingly.

> The elders who direct the affairs of the church well are worthy of double honour, especially those whose work is preaching and teaching. 18 For Scripture says, 'Do not muzzle an ox while it is treading out the grain,' [a] and 'The worker deserves his wages.' (1Timothy 5:17-18, NIV)

The apostle Paul was very specific when he was writing to Timothy. He said serve well, not serve a little. He was referring to those who served the church as pastors/elders/overseers. God's people should pay their pastors generously, although no specific amount should be given. Of course, it is not God's plan for pastors to defraud their sheep or for churches to neglect their pastors. All pastors are to be honoured. However, two kinds of pastors are worthy of "double honour" (v.17):

1. The elders who are good leaders
2. Those who work hard at preaching and teaching

Pastors are not more important than the other members of God's household; however, they are the human leaders of it. The pastor's job is to take care of his church, and it is the church's job to take care of their pastors. Those who proclaim the gospel should make their living by the gospel (1 Corinthians 9:14). The one who is taught the message must share all his good things with the teacher (Galatians 6:6).

2. WE HONOR OUR PASTORS BY DEFENDING THEM

As I mentioned above on the qualification of overseers, the non-negotiable qualification for an elder is that he must have a good reputation with outsiders (1 Timothy 3:7). Apparently, several church leaders attacked the apostle Paul's reputation. My stomach turns when I read his final written words in 2 Timothy 4:14–17:

> Alexander the coppersmith did great harm to me. The Lord will repay him according to his works. Watch out for him yourself because he strongly opposed our words. At my first defense, no one stood by me, but everyone deserted me. May it not be counted against them. But the Lord stood with me and strengthened me, so that the proclamation might be fully made through me and all the Gentiles might hear.

It is the church members' job to not only provide for their pastors but to also protect them from the Alexanders in our churches and communities. Joseph, Moses, David, Jeremiah, and Nehemiah were also criticized publicly. It is not enough to defend our pastors privately. It is each of our jobs to make sure that our pastors are not treated like floor-mats or punching bags.

Pastors also have a moral responsibility to behave honourably. Sometimes it is the very pastors who subject themselves to humiliation and criticism. If this describes you, please repent and do what God has appointed you to. Do not let the world fool you by the glory of men. Be yourself, not anybody else. Do not let people bow down to you. Simple African cultural respect is enough but making yourself a God on earth by pre-texting the Word of God and taking it out of context is a sin.

Join me in defending our pastors against accusers, whether human or demonic.

3. WE HONOR OUR PASTORS BY RESPECTING AND HAVING CONFIDENCE IN THEM

> Now we ask you, brothers, to give respect to those who laboured among you and lead you in the Lord and admonish you. (1Thessalonians 5:12).

> Have confidence in your leaders and submit to their authority, because they keep watch over you as those who must give an account. Do this so that their work will be a joy, not a burden, for that would be of no benefit to you. (Hebrews 13:17)

I have told pastors for years that if you do the best you can, the church will do the best that they can to take care of you. Honestly, that has been the case most of the time but not all the time. In the countries I have visited and preached, sometimes the pastors did not do the best they could, while the church did. Other times, the pastors did the best they could, but the church did not step up. Why is that? Because we are a family and families make mistakes. It seems to take less effort to point out someone's weaknesses than their strengths. I urge you to read the Word of God and know where these pastors' limitations are. Have confidence in them if they are teachable. Regard them as your gate keepers, not your lords. Love them as your spiritual leaders, not your catch 22 or your secret blessings.

In conclusion, it is God's wish that our elderly people/parents be given their utmost respect and honour. The Bible is very clear about such a command. Honoring your father and mother does not only imply your parents but people older than you. God created all people differently for reasons and purposes we may not understand. Regardless of how we perceive other people, they are God's creations. Therefore, it is God's will for us to show respect to everyone.

Use these Bible verses below to be reminded why it is important to show respect to everyone.

> So in everything, do to others what you would have them do to you, for this sums up the Law and the Prophets." Here are a few Bible verses on this topic. (Matthew 7:12)
>
> Be devoted to one another in love. Honour one another above yourselves. (Romans 12:10)
>
> Do nothing out of selfish ambition or vain conceit. Rather, in humility value others above yourselves. (Philippians 2:3)
>
> In everything set them an example by doing what is good. In your teaching show integrity, seriousness. (Titus 2:7)
>
> Show proper respect to everyone, love the family of believers, fear God, honour the emperor. (1 Peter 2:17)
>
> Even as I try to please everyone in every way. For I am not seeking my own good but the good of many, so that they may be saved. (1 Corinthians 10:33)

How Do We Honour And Respect Our Elders, Including Our Pastors?

A new command I give you: Love one another. As I have loved you, so you must love one another. 35 By this everyone will know that you are my disciples, if you love one another. (John 13:34-35)

Rebuke not an elder, but intreat him as a father; [and] the younger men as brethren; 2 The elder women as mothers; the younger as sisters, with all purity. (1 Timothy 5:1-2)

Hear counsel, and receive instruction, that thou mayest be wise in thy latter end. (Proverbs 19:20)

Obey them that have the rule over you, and submit yourselves: for they watch for your souls, as they that must give account, that they may do it with joy, and not with grief: for that [is] unprofitable for you. (Hebrews 13:17)

Likewise, ye younger, submit yourselves unto the elder. Yea, all [of you] be subject one to another and be clothed with humility: for God resist the proud, and giveth grace to the humble. (1 Peter 5:5)

Children, obey your parents in the Lord: for this is right. (Ephesians 6:1)

Thou shalt rise up before the hoary head, and honour the face of the old man, and fear thy God: I am the LORD. (Leviticus 19:32)

Then said he unto the disciples, It is impossible but that offences will come: but woe [unto him], through whom they come! (Luke 17:1-37). Read more on your own.

And it came to pass, that when Isaac was old, and his eyes were dim, so that he could not see, he called Esau his eldest son, and said unto him, my son: and he said unto him, Behold, [here am] I. (Genesis 27:1-46)

Read More:
Ruth 1:1-22
Genesis 5:1-32
Proverbs 19:2
2 Samuel 1:1-27

Notes

CHAPTER 5

What Are Vanity and Eternity?

To answer this question, a few other pastors and I have preached a series of messages as a means of teaching in-depth what vanity and eternity mean. Relax and enjoy the gospel ride!

PART 1: Definition and Introduction — delivered by Pastor Elizabeth Fornah

Introduction

> Yet God has made everything beautiful for its own time. He has planted eternity in the human heart, but even so, people cannot see the whole scope of God's work from beginning to end. (Ecclesiastes 3:11)

> Then I considered all that my hands had done and the toil I had expended in doing it, and behold, all was vanity and a striving after wind, and there was nothing to be gained under the sun. (Ecclesiastes 2:11)

What Are Vanity and Eternity?

These scriptures are telling us that God has planted eternity in the human heart, which means we can never be satisfied with earthly pleasures and pursuits. Because we are created in God's image, we have the following traits:

1. We have a spiritual thirst
2. We have eternal value
3. Nothing but only the eternal God can satisfy us. He has built in us a restless yearning for the kind of perfect world that can only be found in His perfect rule

In Ecclesiastes 2:11, Solomon summarized his many attempts to find life's meaning as "chasing the wind as it passes, but we can't catch hold of it or keep it." In all our accomplishments, even the big ones, our good feelings are only temporary. Secondly, our self-worth and peace are not found in these accomplishments but far beyond them is the love of God. Think about what you consider worthwhile in your life. Where do you invest your energy, time, and money? Will you one day look back and say: "These things were a mere chasing of the wind"?

Definition of Eternity and Vanity.

What is Eternity? Eternity [12] in common parlance is an infinitely long period of time. In classical philosophy, however, eternity is defined as what exists outside time, while sempiternity is the concept that corresponds to the colloquial definition of eternity. Noun: infinite or unending time. synonyms: ever, all time, perpetuity, a state to which time has no application; timelessness. In theology it talks about endless life after death. "Immortal souls destined for eternity."

Synonyms: the afterlife, everlasting life, life after death, the life to come, the life hereafter, the hereafter, the world hereafter, the afterworld, the next world, the beyond, heaven. Immortality is the ability to live forever or eternal life.

What Is Vanity?

Vanity is the excessive belief in one's own abilities or attractiveness to others. Prior to the 14th century, it did not have such narcissistic undertones and merely meant futility. The related term vainglory is now often seen as an archaic synonym for vanity but originally meant boasting in vain, i.e. unjustified boasting. Although glory is now seen as having a predominantly positive meaning, the Latin word *gloria* roughly means

---

[12] Oxford English dictionary – Defines eternity as common parlance of long period of time.

boasting and was often used as a negative criticism. Vanity of a person is seen as having an overestimation of yourself, abilities, looks or other attributes that make you have an excessive belief in your own abilities or attractiveness to others. Perhaps this is the reason a certain piece of bedroom furniture is called a "vanity." It has a mirror and focuses on the person looking into it.

What does the Bible say about vanity and eternity?

The Bible has a lot to say about vanity and eternity as we shall see:

> The end of all things is near. Therefore, be clear-minded and self-controlled, so you can pray. Above all, love each other deeply, because love covers over a multitude of sins. Offer hospitality to one another without grumbling. Each one should use whatever gift he has received to serve others, faithfully administering God's grace in its various forms. If anyone speaks, he should do it as one speaking the very words of God. If anyone serves, he should do it with the strength God provides, so that in all things God may be praised through Jesus Christ. To him be the glory and the power forever and ever. Amen. (1 Peter 4:7-11)

Vanity is an emptiness or uselessness of things. Solomon wrote more about vanity than any other author in the Bible, more so, in Ecclesiastes where vanity is mentioned 32 of the 35 times in the Bible. One such example of the futility or vanity of riches is when "A man to whom God gives wealth, possessions, and honour, so that he lacks nothing of all that he desires; yet, God does not give him power to enjoy them, but a stranger enjoys them. This is vanity; it is a grievous evil" (Ecclesiastes 6:2). "Sometimes a person who has toiled with wisdom and knowledge and skill must leave everything to be enjoyed by someone who did not toil for it. This also is vanity and a great evil" (Ecclesiastes 2:21).

Vanity

Everyone knows the saying, "Pride comes before a fall." In today's world of selfies, vanity, pride and narcissism seem to run rampant. However, it is really a symptom of insecurity, loneliness, and a desire to be loved by those around us. We always want to put our best face forward, so everyone around us sees our favourable side. Unfortunately, being so concerned about our appearance or what others think of us is not worth it in the end. The Bible has something to say about this, so here are my top Bible verses about vanity.

> The words of the Preacher, the son of David, king in Jerusalem. Vanity of vanities, says the Preacher, vanity of vanities! All is vanity. What does man gain by all the toil at which he toils under the sun? A generation goes, and a generation comes, but the earth remains forever. The sun rises, and the sun goes down, and hastens to the place where it rises. (Ecclesiastes 1:1-18)

What Are Vanity and Eternity?

> Now this I say and testify in the Lord, that you must no longer walk as the Gentiles do, in the futility of their minds. (Ephesians 4:17)

> Keep your life free from love of money, and be content with what you have, for he has said, "I will never leave you nor forsake you. (Hebrews 13:5)

Today's culture puts a great deal of emphasis on beauty and outward appearances. Movies and magazines even try to tell us what is beautiful and politically correct. Being vain just seems to be the norm. However, the Lord reminds us in this verse that charm and beauty are only vanity and temporary. In God's view, a woman or any person who fears Him, is even more appealing and worthy to be praised. In other words, what is on the inside of a person is more important than what is on the outside.

> He who loves money will not be satisfied with money, nor he who loves wealth with his income; this also is vanity. (Ecclesiastes 5:10)

I included this verse in my teaching because money has often led people to feel a sense of importance and arrogance. These are synonymous with vanity because those who believe they are better than others or anything else are just setting themselves up for a fall. Nothing—not looks or money—can make a person truly happy. "Vanity of vanities, says the preacher; all is vanity." (Ecclesiastes 12:8)

What does the Bible say about eternity?

The Bible says that everybody will "live" for eternity. Some will have eternal life and some eternal death.

> Do not marvel at this; for the hour is coming in which all who are in the graves will hear His voice and come forth- those who have done good, to the resurrection of life, and those who have done evil, to the resurrection of condemnation. (John 5:28-29)

The Bible also tells us what we must do to have eternal life:

> For God so loved the world that He gave His only begotten Son, that whoever believes in Him should not perish but have everlasting life. For God did not send His Son into the world to condemn the world, but that the world through Him might be saved. "He who believes in Him is not condemned; but he who does not believe is condemned already, because he has not believed in the name of the only begotten Son of God. (John 3:16-18)

This message of good news comes to a focus in this verse. God's love is not static or self-centered. It reaches out and draws others in. Here, God sets the pattern of true love, which is the basis of all love relationships. When we love someone dearly, we are willing to give freely to the point of self-sacrifice. God paid dearly with His own Son. So in actual fact, what we value determines what we do. Not just what we do as a profession but every action and thought. The world has its own ideas about what is valuable: money/possessions, status/power, security/comfort, and legacy. But as the world defines these things, they are not transferable to eternity. As the old saying goes, "You can't take it with you."

Things with eternal value are, by definition, valuable forever. Our time on earth is very short, but what we do here will affect our condition in eternity. In that never-ending life, we will either be tormented in hell or enjoying God's new heaven and new earth. The things of this world will pass away (1 John 2:17). The world and its desires pass away but whoever does the will of God lives forever. It is encouraging to note that the Word and people will not pass away. But there is that catch, doing the will of GOD.

God's great commandment reflects this: love God; love people (Matthew 22:34-40). Only God and people have eternal value. Hence, our actions and efforts should be motivated by the effort to love God and people. How does this compare with the world?

Money/possessions: Wealth is fleeting; we will not maintain our earthly socio-economic class in eternity. Our money, then, must be subservient to the Great Commandment—how can we use money to love and worship God? Help people. How does money get in the way of loving God and others? How does God want each one of us as individuals to use money to honour Him? Money can make it hard to follow Christ (Mark 10:23), but it can also be used to serve others (Acts 9:36).

Status/power: Worldly respect and power have been coveted by men since Lamech in Genesis Chapter 4. It makes us feel validated when others affirm our worth. God's view of respect is different. We should strive to earn others' respect only insofar as it brings glory to God and draws others to Him. We are to live in peace with others (Romans 12:18) because it's healthy for the church. As a child, Jesus "increased in wisdom and in stature and in favour with God and man" (Luke 2:52) because He honoured God, not for the purposes of controlling people.

Education/knowledge: Throughout the Bible, passages highlight the importance of education. Psalm 119, the longest chapter in the Bible, is dedicated to contemplating God's law. God Himself gave Solomon wisdom (1 Kings 3:5-12). God gave Daniel and his friends "learning and skill in all literature and wisdom" (Daniel 1:17). Knowledge of the law was part of Paul's pedigree of accomplishments (Philippians 3:5). But Jesus, Solomon, and Daniel knew that wisdom was useless unless it was used in the service of God.

Before his conversion, Paul used his knowledge to persecute Christians. After, he considered his knowledge rubbish "because of the surpassing worth of knowing Christ Jesus my Lord" (Philippians 3:8). Knowledge and education are good only if used for eternal purposes.

Security/comfort: Our desires for safety and ease, like other worldly things, are not necessarily bad. The Old Testament shows that such things are blessings. But in the church age, we're called to postpone these longings for just a little while. Several places in the New Testament (John 15:18-19; 2 Timothy 3:12; 1 Peter 4:3-4) say that Christians should expect to be persecuted. But that persecution is directly connected with things of eternal value. In fact, Jesus said that the fact we are persecuted shows that we value eternity (John 15:18-19). We cannot be perfectly safe in this world; God does not promise to protect us or our families from harm. But if harm comes because we had the integrity to love God and others, it is "a gracious thing in the sight of God" (1 Peter 2:20).

Legacy: The closest we can come to things of eternal value on earth is our legacy—our influence on the world that lasts after we die. But even this is fleeting. Solomon built a mighty temple that was destroyed within hundreds of years. The Bible does give examples of eternal, spiritual legacies: an act of worship to Christ (Matthew 26:6-13), the people we reach (2 Corinthians 3:2-3), sincere faith that inspires others (2 Timothy 1:5).

The only things we will be able to take to eternity are our relationship with God and the people we reached with the gospel. Things on this earth are merely tools we use to prepare for eternity. If we can remember this, we will gather things of eternal value. It is our witness, not our wealth that will matter. Finally, I cannot conclude without giving people the opportunity to surrender their lives to Jesus Christ or repent of any sin that has to do with vanity. Have you in one way or the other considered the world's ideas about what is valuable? Are money/possessions, status/power, security/comfort, and legacy more important than people, God, and His Word? If so, I invite you to pray the following prayer:

Father, in the name of Jesus, I confess I have sinned against You for following my heart's desires and earthly benefits. As of today, reject and renounce any of those practices and thoughts. Lord, give me a heart of flesh, not one of stone, so I can serve you more diligently. In Jesus' precious name. I pray. Amen.

5.1 Can possession and pride lead us to eternity?

The emphatic answer to this is no. See the message below delivered by a wonderful man of God.

PART 2: VANITY AND ETERNITY - POSSESSION AND PRIDE

> At the end of the days I, Nebuchadnezzar, lifted my eyes to heaven, and my reason returned to me, and I blessed the Most High, and praised and honoured him who lives forever, for his dominion is an everlasting dominion, and his kingdom endures from generation to generation. (Daniel 4:34)

INTRODUCTION

We are continuing with our series on vanity and eternity started by our father, Apostle Francis. Today, we will be focusing particularly on pride and possessions. These are some of the main strongholds the Enemy has used to keep the world in bondage. Today, I pray that with this message, the Enemy will be completely exposed and rendered powerless when it comes to these areas in your life. We will be looking at what it is, as well as some examples of the pitfalls, when we fall prey to these strongholds in the Word of God.

PRIDE

So what is pride? Definition: a feeling of deep pleasure or satisfaction derived from one's own achievements, the achievements of one's close associates or from qualities or possessions that are widely admired.

The danger here is that pride feeds you with a deep sense of self. It makes you focus all your energy and attention only on yourself. It can make you become a narcissist (excessive preoccupation with oneself). In a condition like that, you fail to appreciate or notice what others do. If they do better than you, rather than celebrate them, you are filled with jealously, conceit, and hatred. In that condition, God is dethroned from receiving any glory from your life. This is a perfect recipe for disaster! "When pride comes, then comes disgrace, but with humility comes wisdom" (Proverbs 11:2).

Being a disciple means you are ever learning. You never reach a stage where you know everything or you believe you are equal or greater than your master. True disciples are just like small children who always look up to their teachers seeking more knowledge. Their hunger and eagerness make their teachers want to share more with them. They never look at themselves even to see how much they have learnt.

The "I" mentality is not found in a disciple but is always in prideful people trying to justify their own actions. In their own eyes, they are always right. How can you ever learn or be corrected if you are always right? Only God is perfect!

Examples of looking at self:

1. Genesis 3:8-1 2 ~~Adam~~ because of self-pride could not admit that he was wrong and blamed everyone else but himself. In his eyes, Eve was wrong and deserved to be punished alone.

2. Ezekiel 28:1-1 0 ~~Being~~ an ally of Israel the King of Tyre grew proud. When God rejects you there is nowhere to hide.

3. Isaiah 14:12-1 7 ~~The~~ fall of Lucifer! Notice how many thoughts he was having about himself from verse16.

The danger of pride is that it makes you feel no one can correct you, not even God. Disloyalty and disobedience are signs of pride.

HOW TO GUARD AGAINST PRIDE

1. Remain humble and God will lift you up (James 4:5-10).

2. Have a teachable spirit. Be willing to learn from anyone God can use. Yes, even from little children who can be used by God to teach us!

3. Acknowledge always when God uses you that it is not you, but it is God in you.

4. Refuse to let people give you the glory or worship you. If angels refuse to be worship when they appeared to man in their magnificence, how much more should we refuse to take any of God's glory for ourselves. Remember He is a jealous God (Acts 14:8-18).

Jesus asked, "Why do you call me good teacher?" (Mark 10:18). Also read Philippians 2:5-11. Although Jesus was God, He humbled Himself, became as a bondservant, and God lifted Him up! God responds to our pride or humility. Pride = fall. Humility = lifting

POSSESSIONS

Definition: the state of having, owning or controlling

God should be honoured even with our possessions. We should recognize that it is a privilege from God to have what we have. We are custodians. He can take our valuables away at any time for His glory.

> When He had called the people to Himself, with His disciples also, He said to them, "Whoever desires to come after Me, let him deny himself, and take up his cross, and follow Me. For whoever desires to save his life will lose it, but whoever loses his life for My sake and the gospel's will save it. For what will it profit a man if he gains the whole world, and loses his own soul? (Mark 8:34-36).

We should always focus on our souls rather than the desires of the flesh.

The question is, how do we glorify God with what we have? Hannah wanted a baby to silence her enemies, not to glorify God. When she finally prayed and committed her possessions (the baby she would have) to God, that is when God answered her prayer (1 Samuel Chapter 1). James 4:1-4 reveals that we ask amiss when we ask for possessions with selfish motives that do nothing for God.

> There is one who scatters yet increases more; And there is one who withholds more than is right, but it leads to poverty. The generous soul will be made rich, and he who waters will also be watered himself. The people will curse him who withholds grain, But blessing will be on the head of him who sells it. (Proverbs 11:24-28, NJKV)

Contrary to what the world teaches, withholding more than what is necessary (excess) actually leads to poverty! Trusting in riches leads to a fall. True prosperity from God is on to generous souls for God can trust them not to be distracted by what they have for they continue to acknowledge that even though God has made them custodians of the wealth for a little while, everything still belongs to God. After all, the word "Lord" means owner, and Jesus Christ is the Lord of lords. Everything we have was made through Him, by Him, and for Him (John Chapter 1 and Colossians Chapter 1).

Job understood this very well. No man has suffered such loss as he did. Everything he owned was gone in one day. The world he knew was finished. Yet, in all of it, Job refused to turn away from God. He glorified Him all the more!

> Now there was a day when his sons and daughters were eating and drinking wine in their oldest brother's house; and a messenger came to Job and said, "The oxen were plowing and the donkeys feeding beside them, when the Sabeans raided them and took them away—indeed they have killed the servants with the edge of the sword; and I alone have escaped to tell you!" While he was still speaking, another also came and said, "The fire of God fell from heaven and burned up the sheep and the servants and consumed them; and I alone have escaped to tell you!" While he was still speaking, another also came

and said, "The Chaldeans formed three bands, raided the camels and took them away, yes, and killed the servants with the edge of the sword; and I alone have escaped to tell you!" While he was still speaking, another also came and said, "Your sons and daughters were eating and drinking wine in their oldest brother's house, and suddenly a great wind came from across the wilderness and struck the four corners of the house, and it fell on the young people, and they are dead; and I alone have escaped to tell you!" Then Job arose, tore his robe, and shaved his head; and he fell to the ground and worshiped. And he said: "Naked I came from my mother's womb, and naked shall I return there. The Lord gave, and the Lord has taken away; Blessed be the name of the Lord." In all this Job did not sin nor charge God with wrong. (Job 1:13-20, NKJV).

Job 1:22 even says that in spite of all this, Job did not sin against God. He understood his greatest treasure wasn't what he had in material possessions. His greatest treasure was his relationship with God.

> Do not lay up for yourselves treasures on earth, where moth and rust destroy and where thieves break in and steal, but lay up for yourselves treasures in heaven, where neither moth nor rust destroys and where thieves do not break in and steal. For where your treasure is, there your heart will be also. (Matthew 6:19-21)

God wants to be loved by you with all your mind, heart, and strength. You cannot worship mammon and God at the same time. You cannot be faithful to both. It's not possible. You will always love one more than the other.

The Devil has successfully misled the world with the illusion of chasing the unattainable dream. You have heard of the phrase, "chasing the American dream." This is the real fake news! No amount of possessions could ever satisfy your soul. The reality is most people typically buy things they don't need with money they don't have to impress people they don't even like.

> And you, O desolate one, what do you mean that you dress in scarlet, that you adorn yourself with ornaments of gold, that you enlarge your eyes with paint? In vain you beautify yourself. Your lovers despise you; they seek your life. (Jeremiah 4:30)

It is not a loss to follow God. Rather, following Him is the truest treasure of all. You gain everything. Our desire should be to obey the first commandment of loving the Lord God with all our hearts, minds, and strength. We worship God, not because of what He can do or what He has but to love Him for who He is. Read Luke 18:24-29. Your sacrifice shall never go unrewarded. Prideful people are very possessive. They never want to give more than they receive. They expect loyalty even when they are unfaithful themselves. Jesus said remove the log in your eye first before trying to remove the twigs in your brothers' eyes (Matthew 7:5)

The rich, young man failed to follow God because of his possessions (Mark 10:18). "Honour the Lord with your possessions" (Proverbs 3:5). Always remember it is God who causes man to acquire wealth (Deuteronomy 8:18, 1 Samuel 2:6-8). In all things, be content in every season God places you. You will preserve your soul and gain eternity (Philippians 4:11-13).

May the Lord bless us and remove pride from our lives. May we never be too focused on what we have or attain it in such a way that we lose God in the process. God is the richest treasure we could ever have. Relax! God's got you! Amen.

5.2 Who do you allow to define your identity and self-image?

PART 3: VANITY AND ETERNITY - IDENTITY AND SELF-IMAGE

So God created man in his own image, in the image of God he created him; male and female he created them (Genesis 1:27, ESV)

Before I formed you in the womb, I knew you, and before you were born I consecrated you; I appointed you a prophet to the nations. (Jeremiah 1:5, ESV)

INTRODUCTION

> But you are a chosen race, a royal priesthood, a holy nation, a people for his own possession, that you may proclaim the excellencies of him who called you out of darkness into his marvelous light. (1 Peter 2:9, ESV)

Knowing our true identities and having a good self-image can certainly be a battle as we live in a world that seeks to define us by its own standards. But it's a battle that when we engage in it could impact everything about us! My question is "How would believing the truth about your new identity in Christ change the way you live?"

Over the course of our lives, each person's identity is being formed through individual experiences, relationships, culture, media, and the world around us. We are constantly seeking to define who we are in any way that we can. The Bible says,

> See what kind of love the Father has given to us, that we should be called children of God; and so, we are. The reason why the world does not know us is that it did not know him. Beloved, we are God's children now, and what we will be has not yet appeared; but we know that when he appears we shall be like him, because we shall see him as he is. And everyone who thus hopes in him purifies himself as he is pure. (1 John 3:1-3)

DEFINING OUR IDENTITY

David Benner, [13] a psychologist and author of the book, *The Gift of Being Yourself*, defines identity as "who we experience ourselves to be—the "I or me" each of us carries within." Often, we feel the pressure to define ourselves through our jobs, financial status, successes, grades, appearances, what other people say about us and many other means. This is where self-image and the I or me comes in to play. Paul made it very clear to Timothy:

> For people will be lovers of self, lovers of money, proud, arrogant, abusive, disobedient to their parents, ungrateful, unholy, heartless, unappeasable, slanderous, without self-control, brutal, not loving good, treacherous, reckless, swollen with conceit, lovers of pleasure rather than lovers of God. (2 Timothy 3:2-4)

But what happens to our identities when we fail to accumulate worldly things, lose someone's favour or become burnt out in our jobs or place of service? The reality starts to kick in when the very foundation of our identity is shaken and altered. The result is we hustle to define ourselves by something or someone else. We end up hopping around for prophecies and words of knowledge. A stable sense of self cannot fully

---

[13] Dr David G Benner and M. Basil Pennington 2015, psychologists and authors of the book The Gift of Being Yourself, The Sacred Call to Self-Discovery (Spiritual Journey) defines identity as "who we experience ourselves to be – the "I or Me" each of us carries within.

exist when we place our identities in external things. If we do this, when circumstances change, our identities constantly change too. This is vanity.

We may receive an overwhelming number of messages telling us to define ourselves by external measures. However, what would it look like to base our identities on the way God sees us? Benner states that "An identity grounded in God would mean that when we think of who we are, the first thing that would come to mind is our status as someone who is deeply loved by God."

The Bible tells us that if we are in Christ, we are new creations. The old has passed away; behold, the new has come (2 Corinthians 5:17).

How would viewing yourself as a new creation in this manner change the way you live? What are some obstacles you will face in doing this?

The first thing we should consider in answering such questions is how God sees us. It is very important to know how God sees us, what He thinks about us, and what His desires are for us. How can you trust somebody you aren't sure is looking out for your best interest? How can you freely put your life in the hands of somebody you perceive may use you and not be trustworthy? That is one of the fundamental reasons why Christians today have a hard time trusting God. They know little about Him. They do not understand how He sees us and that He has good things in mind for us! Therefore, studying about how God sees us and getting it down into our spirits that He really does love us, desires good things for us, and cares for us, is vital to our ability to trust Him. "For I know the plans I have for you, declares the Lord, plans for welfare and not for evil, to give you a future and a hope" (Jeremiah 29:11).

The fact is that until you know in your heart God really does love and care for you, it's going to be difficult to believe His promises for you. They just won't make much sense! I like how Benny Hinn once said that when you believe in God's power, "God can." However, when you believe in His love, "God will." I felt the Holy Spirit saying to me, "Believe in me; believe in my love for you." Then a verse came to me, saying, "The Lord delights in those who fear him, who put their hope in his unfailing love" (Psalm 147:11, NIV).

One of the richest passages about identity in the Bible is found in Ephesians 1:3-14. In this passage, Paul addresses the church in Ephesus explaining the new identity given to those who are in Christ. They will have all the benefits of knowing God, being chosen for salvation, being adopted as His children, forgiveness, insight, the gift of the Spirit, the power to do God's will and the hope of living forever with Christ. This is eternity.

According to Ephesians Chapter 1, we have been blessed with every spiritual blessing; we have been chosen, adopted, redeemed, forgiven, grace-lavished, and unconditionally loved and accepted. We are pure, blameless, and forgiven. We have received the hope of spending eternity with God. When we are in Christ, these aspects of our identities can never be altered by what we do.

Many obstacles often hinder us from gaining eternal life when we focus on the tags and labels people tend to put on us. A gap exists between intellectually knowing these truths about who God says we are and living it out. This can be affected by how we see ourselves, life experiences, and the ways we allow the world to define us. Knowing who you are in Christ is vital to your spiritual growth, healing, and deliverance. One of the essential things that I look for in the people to whom I minister is their self-image. If they have a problem in this area of their lives, the process of inner healing and deliverance can be hindered. Overcoming this roadblock is essential to moving forward smoothly and efficiently to get rid of bondages in people's lives.

To live out the fullness of our new identity in Christ, we must determine what is hindering us from doing so. This varies from person to person. Many times, a false belief wedges itself between how God defines us and seeing ourselves in the same light and how others define us. When we begin to feel guilty, we need to get to the root of the problem and address it with God's Word. What does God's Word say about our guilt? It tells us that if we confess our sins and forsake it, we are forgiven and cleansed of whatever kind of unrighteousness we've committed. When we choose to believe that over how we feel, our feelings will change because they are merely the fruit of our thoughts and beliefs. In this case, our feelings were wrong because our beliefs were wrong. Remember, feelings are just the fruit of our thoughts and beliefs. If we feel wrong, then it wouldn't hurt to stop and ask ourselves what we believe. Do we believe that when a man confesses his sin and believes upon Christ that he is forgiven? Or do we, in the back of our minds, wonder if we've sinned too badly or if we need to do something before we can be forgiven? Our feelings can be of a greater benefit when they reveal what we really believe under the surface.

It is important to be balanced when dealing with our feelings. I don't think it's healthy to completely ignore them, but I can assure you, it is not healthy to go by our feelings either. The key is to learn how to discern what our feelings are really telling us. Then we can get to the root of the problem. Feelings of guilt, for example, do not necessarily mean we are indeed guilty. Rather, that our beliefs are not rooted and grounded on God's Word as they ought to. A typical example of the opposite of "pure and blameless" would be "impure, stained or guilty." Perhaps a life experience has caused you to feel impure or guilty, so you believe God sees you this way. You then create and live out an identity based on your actions and beliefs, which are contrary to how God sees you.

We must fight against dirty consciences because the blood of Jesus Christ has done the work for us as stated in Hebrews 9:14: "How much more shall the blood of Christ, who through the eternal Spirit offered himself without spot to God, purge your conscience from dead works to serve the living God?" To fight against these false beliefs and dirty consciences, we must discover the exact belief we are allowing to form our identities. When reflecting on the passage in Ephesians 1, some false beliefs we may live out are:

- Rejected instead of accepted
- In bondage instead of redeemed
- Under the law instead of covered by grace
- Feeling orphaned instead of adopted, and so on

Living out one of those identities as opposed to our new identity in Christ affects our behaviours. This begins to lead us to self-conceptualization of things and blaming people for our misconceptions. If we still think we are under the law, we may think we must "do" more for God to be right with Him. We may bury ourselves in ministry, service or other good works to feel as though we're in good standing with God instead of resting in Christ's work on the cross.

HOW DO WE DEAL WITH FALSE BELIEFS?

To deal with false beliefs, you must recognize that they are false beliefs. Once we know this, then we ought to surrender them to God in repentance, which means in Greek "to change one's mind."

> Because, if you confess with your mouth that Jesus is Lord and believe in your heart that God raised him from the dead, you will be saved. For with the heart one believes and is justified, and with the mouth one confesses and is saved. (Romans 10:9-10)

After repentance, we must replace the lie with the truth found in Scripture. "If we confess our sins, he is faithful and just to forgive us our sins and to cleanse us from all unrighteousness" (1 John 1:9). Sometimes the lie is connected to a very real, painful experience. Take some time to grieve over the experience and invite God into the place of brokenness. After you have surrendered the lie to God, pray that He will help you believe the truth about who He says you are and make you aware of the times you are not believing it. Then, make the choice to believe it!

We may not always "feel" forgiven or blameless, but the truth is, God sees us that way. This is where faith comes in.

> For though we walk in the flesh, we are not waging war according to the flesh. For the weapons of our warfare are not of the flesh but have divine power to destroy strongholds. We destroy arguments and every lofty opinion raised against the knowledge of God and take every thought captive to obey Christ. (2 Corinthians 10:3-5)

God has given us everything we need to demolish strongholds or false beliefs, and He empowers us to do so.

In conclusion, we should be viewing ourselves as God sees us, not as the world tags and labels us. If we live out our identities based on how God sees us, we would no longer feel the need to find our worth in our external circumstances. We would find total freedom to live in a confident and stable manner, instead of changing who we are based on others, the jobs we have or don't have, how we see ourselves, and all the other ways we try to define our significance. It would give us the opportunity to experience God's unconditional love for us in new and fresh ways. And it would allow us to confidently and boldly share His love with others.

Be mindful of the fact that life, however, is not always a success story. There are times when a person has to face the disappointments and frustrations of a task or a life that has been messed up. Remember that man is finite. Man can never fully comprehend the work of God.

> When I applied my heart to know wisdom, and to see the business that is done on earth, how neither day nor night do one's eyes see sleep, then I saw all the work of God, that man cannot find out the work that is done under the sun. However, much man may toil in seeking, he will not find it out. Even though a wise man claims to know, he cannot find it out. (Ecclesiastes 8:16-17)

So all is vanity. Your identity in Christ Jesus is perfect and the best.

PART 4: VANITY AND ETERNITY - KNOWLEDGE, EDUCATION, AND CULTURE

For the LORD gives wisdom; from his mouth come knowledge and understanding. (Proverbs 2:6)

The heart of the discerning acquires knowledge, for the ears of the wise seek it out. (Proverbs 18:15)

And how from infancy you have known the Holy Scriptures, which are able to make you wise for salvation through faith in Christ Jesus. 16All Scripture is God-breathed and is useful for teaching, rebuking, correcting and training in righteousness. (2 Timothy 3:15-16)

For the protection of wisdom is like the protection of money, and the advantage of knowledge is that wisdom preserves the life of him who has it. (Ecclesiastes 7:12)

After this I looked, and there before me was a great multitude that no one could count, from every nation, tribe, people and language, standing before the throne and before the Lamb. They were wearing white robes and were holding palm branches in their hands. 10And they cried out in a loud voice: "Salvation belongs to our God, who sits on the throne, and to the Lamb. (Revelation 7:9-10)

What is Knowledge?

Knowledge [14] is a familiarity, awareness or understanding of someone or something such as facts, information, descriptions or skills acquired through experience or education by perceiving, discovering or learning.

What is Education?

Education is the process of facilitating learning or the acquisition of knowledge, skills, values, beliefs, and habits. Educational methods include storytelling, discussion, teaching, training, and directed research. Education frequently takes place under the guidance of educators, but learners may also educate themselves.

What is Culture?

Culture is the characteristics and knowledge of a particular group of people defined by everything from language, religion, cuisine, social habits, music, and arts. Through God's Word we gain an understanding that God is the one who gives the gift of knowledge (an understanding or awareness of something). However, the Lord grants knowledge to those who have an honest relationship with Him. This collection of Bible verses gives insight into the value of knowledge and the path to gaining it.

---

[14] Collins Gem Thesaurus; A-Z definitions of words (major new edition).

Education/knowledge: Throughout the Bible, passages highlight the importance of education. Psalm 119, the longest chapter in the Bible, is dedicated to contemplating God's law. God, Himself gave Solomon wisdom (1 Kings 3:5-12). He gave Daniel and his friends "learning and skill in all literature and wisdom" (Daniel 1:17). Knowledge of the law was part of Paul's pedigree of accomplishments (Philippians 3:5). But Jesus, Solomon, and Daniel knew that wisdom was useless unless it was used in the service of God. Before his conversion, Paul used his knowledge to persecute Christians. After, he considered his knowledge rubbish "because of the surpassing worth of knowing Christ Jesus my Lord" (Philippians 3:8). Knowledge and education are good only if used for eternal purposes.

> Moses was educated in all the learning of the Egyptians, and he was a man of power in words and deeds. (Acts 7:22)

> As for these four youths, God gave them knowledge and intelligence in every branch of literature and wisdom; Daniel even understood all kinds of visions and dreams. (Daniel 1:17)

1. There are basically two kingdoms: a kingdom of light and a kingdom of darkness. It seems strange to have those who walk in darkness educate children of light. It doesn't fit.

2. If Jesus Christ is Lord, then He is Lord of all. We cannot divide things into secular and sacred.

3. All truth is God's truth, and God's Word sheds light on our path. Only in His light can we see light. Education is not focused on possibilities but on certainties found in God's Word.

4. Deuteronomy Chapter 6 tells parents that, in all they do, they should provide a godly education 24/7.

5. Three key institutions that shape a child are the home, the church, and the school. Children are served best when all three institutions point them in the same direction.

6. Only an education that has the liberty to address the whole child: social, intellectual, emotional, physical, and spiritual reaches the possibility of excellence.

7. The best preparation for effective service is to be well-grounded in one's mind before direct engagement of the culture.

Culture and Christianity [15]

At the close of the twentieth century, American evangelicals found themselves in a diverse, pluralistic culture. Many ideas vie for attention and allegiance. These ideas, philosophies or world views are the products of philosophical and cultural changes. Such changes have come to define our culture. For example, pluralism can mean that all world views are

---

[15] Eckermann, A. K et al (2015) Binan Goong, Bridging cultures and Ryan Nelson, (2015) Views on the Relationship between Christianity and Culture.

correct and that it is intolerable to state otherwise; secularism reigns; absolutes have ceased to exist; facts can only be stated in the realm of science, not religion; evangelical Christianity has become nothing more than a troublesome oddity amidst diversity. It is clear, therefore, that western culture is suffering; it is ill. Since the term culture is central in this discussion, it deserves particular attention and definition.

Even though the concept behind the word is ancient, and it is used frequently in many different contexts, its actual meaning is elusive and often confusing. Culture does not refer to a particular level of life. This level, sometimes referred to as "high culture" is certainly an integral part of the definition, but it is not the central focus. For example, "the arts" are frequently identified with culture in the minds of many. More often than not, there is a qualitative difference between what is a part of "high culture" and other segments of culture, but these distinctions are not our concern at this time. Christians are to observe and analyse culture and make decisions regarding our proper actions and reactions within it.

We are privileged today to live in a world of many cultures, and the Bible verses on cultural diversity reminded us that it's really something we notice more than God. We can all learn a lot about each other's cultures, but as Christians, we live as one in Jesus Christ. Living in faith together is more about not noticing gender, race or culture. Living in faith as a body of

Christ is about loving God, period. Here are some Bible verses on cultural diversity:

> And foreigners who bind themselves to the Lord to minister to him, to love the name of the Lord, and to be his servants, all who keep the Sabbath without desecrating it and who hold fast to my covenant—7 these I will bring to my holy mountain and give them joy in my house of prayer. Their burnt offerings and sacrifices will be accepted on my altar; for my house will be called a house of prayer for all nations." 8 The Sovereign Lord declares—he who gathers the exiles of Israel: "I will gather still others to them besides those already gathered. (Isaiah 56:6-8, NIV)

The vanity of culture

> Do not be conformed to this world, but be transformed by the renewal of your mind, that by testing you may discern what is the will of God, what is good and acceptable and perfect. (Romans 12:2)

HOW DOES THE DEVIL USE ALL OF THESE TO HINDER OUR SPIRITUAL GROWTH, FINANCIAL BREAK-THROUGH, EDUCATIONAL GROWTH, JOB ACQUISITION, STABILITY, AND SOBRIETY?

Satan cannot read our minds; he can influence our thoughts. Thus, the Bible instructs us to "Put on the full armour of God so that you can take your stand against the devil's schemes" (Ephesians 6:11, NIV). Without it, you are a guaranteed casualty in the invisible war. With it, you are invincible. Spiritual warfare is waged against invisible beings that personify the extremities of evil and their weapons are spiritual, not physical.

1. He may corrupt your mind, steer you away from the simplicity of Christ and His gospel (2 Corinthians 11:3) and make you become proud.

When pride comes, then comes disgrace, but with humility comes wisdom. (Proverbs 11:2)

Pride goes before destruction, a haughty spirit before a fall. (Proverbs 16:18)

To fear the LORD is to hate evil; I hate pride and arrogance, evil behaviour and perverse speech. (Proverbs 8:13)

2. He may wrestle against you, fighting against your progress in Christ (Ephesians 6:12). He will fight against your prosperity in everything.

3. He may harass you with some form of fleshly affliction and torment (2 Corinthians 12:7).

4. He may blind you spiritually, so you cannot see your wrong (2 Corinthians 4:4). The god of this world has blinded the minds of unbelievers to keep them from seeing the light of the gospel of

the glory of Christ who is the image of God. "Let them alone; they are blind guides. And if the blind lead the blind, both will fall into a pit" (Matthew 15:14).

No matter what you are going through, your delay is not a curse. When your breakthrough comes, the entire world will know. Be blessed. I hope this answers your questions on vanity and eternity.

Notes

CHAPTER 6

Church Hoppers and Prophecy Shoppers

Does church hopping and prophecy shopping bring glory to God and if not, what happens to those caught up in such practices?

Here are a few facts to answer your questions on issues surrounding church hoppers and prophecy shoppers. Relax and enjoy the gospel ride for free.

INTRODUCTION

Many people wonder why their friends and families go around from church to church consulting one pastor or prophet to the other. Well, this message will probably answer some of those concerns. As we all know, many Christians today are seeking miracles and quick fixes to their self-created problems or generational curses that have been ignited through their deliberate sins after being born again. Isaiah 61:1-2, says:

> The Spirit of the Lord God is upon me, because the Lord has anointed me to bring good news to the poor; he has sent me to bind up the brokenhearted, to proclaim liberty to the captives, and the opening of

the prison to those who are bound; to proclaim the year of the Lord's favor, and the day of vengeance of our God; to comfort all who mourn

This is confirmed in Luke 4:18-19.

The reason I stated these two scriptures is to let those prophecy and church hoppers know that God, who is in His Son Jesus Christ, came in the form of man to do exactly what the prophets have said. So, the best way to get your prophecy and direction is to seek the face of God Himself. Baby Christians should be conversant with the Bible, which is the sword of the Spirit. In this message, I will touch on very sensitive issues that may make people think they have been targeted. By that I mean, expose their cunning tricks and signs to compromise pastors and prophets.

> Let us not give up meeting together, as some are in the habit of doing, but let us encourage one another—and all the more as you see the Day approaching." Sometimes people church-hop or prophecy hop to avoid getting too deeply involved with any one congregation, but that defeats the purpose of the body of Christ which is, as Hebrews notes, to "encourage one another. (Hebrews 10:25)

We can't encourage those we don't spend time getting to know, and we cannot be encouraged by other Christians if they are essentially strangers to us.

WHO ARE CHURCH HOPPERS OR PROPHECY SHOPPERS?

These are people who go from church to church and prophets or pastors to pastors seeking to be given favourable and positive prophecies even though they are living compromising and sinful lives. In real life, we call them expert Christians who, without doubt, will seek to lure pastors or prophets to compromise their status by giving them unexpected tithes or gifts that will make them dance to their tune. This kind of spirit is manipulative and destructive. Such people carry Jezebel and Ahab spirits and must be confronted. Jezebel's hold cannot be tolerated over any ministry. It must be broken. Jesus had some incredibly stern and intense words for the church of Thyatira. In Revelation 2:20 it says, "Nevertheless, I have this against you: You tolerate that woman Jezebel, who calls herself a prophet. By her teaching she misleads my servants into sexual immorality and the eating of food sacrificed to idols" (NIV).

In the Bible, Jezebel was a woman who married King Ahab. Jezebel worshipped Astarte the demonic goddess known as the Queen of Heaven and the god Baal. Other names for Astarte are Ashteroth and Ashtoreth. She coerced her husband to abandon Yahweh and do the same. Jesus understood the power and influence of the spirit of Jezebel and wanted this spirit broken off the church in Thyatira. He plainly said that these people tolerated Jezebel. The English definition of the word "tolerate" gives insight into why Jesus made such a statement against this church.

To tolerate means to allow the existence, presence, practice or act of (something that one does not necessarily like or agree with) without prohibition or hindrance; permit.

What makes this so significant is the fact that the spirit of Jezebel was not agreed with, but also, she was not interfered with. The leaders of Thyatira allowed her to manifest in their church. This was tragic! Jezebel will never be conquered unless she is confronted. It was so terrible to Jesus that He said, "I am holding this against you." We must never tolerate what Jesus wants us to obliterate.

Church hoppers and prophecy shoppers hide behind what they do and pretend to be right in what they are doing. They can even quote you scriptures and pretext them to suit their sins. They even call that the grace of God. Romans 6:1-4 tells us that grace does not give you permission to sin. Going from one prophet to the other and one pastor to the other looking for prophecies and words of knowledge to cover up your sins does not work in God's kingdom. Romans 11:6, also tells us that grace is not based on human performance.

Jesus held this intolerant attitude against this church because He was fully cognizant of the damage the spirit of Jezebel could inflict. In the same way He wanted the church in Thyatira to be aware of the spirit of Jezebel, He wants us to be as well. But it is not enough to just be aware of her; she must be dealt with. To do so, you must:

1. Allow God to deal with you before you deal with anyone else. As we learnt in the school of intercessors, we must allow God to do unto us first what He wants us to do for others.

    This is of extreme importance. When you come against this spirit, it is important that your heart is pure before the Lord. Ask God to guide, lead, and direct you. Search your heart and empty yourself of all anger and bitterness toward the person you are confronting.

2. If you are not a spiritual leader, find one. Recognize your own potential for operating in the Jezebel spirit. It is imperative for you to walk in submission to a God-ordained spiritual leader. You must come to your leader first and then submit to his/her counsel. It is best if your leader confronts the person dominated by this spirit with you. If this leader says not to approach the person you believe to be under the control of Jezebel, then don't approach him/her. Realize you have done what you could and should do and continue to make this a matter of prayer.

3. Approach this person in humility and determination. Pride is an incredible hindrance to all the work of the Lord. Be led by the law of love. If you pridefully approach this person filled with a religious

spirit, you have lost before you even started. This encounter must find its very roots in prayer. Personally, submit to the Holy Spirit, and come not only as a revealer but also as a healer. Be determined but don't be detrimental to this person's life and walk. Your issue is with Jezebel, not the person. Meekness, gentleness, and humility will bring you the victory.

4. Pray, pray, and pray again. Pray for the person caught by the Jezebel spirit and all Jezebel influences. Prayer binds Jezebel. Declare in faith that every chain of control that this spirit has over the lives of people is destroyed and broken. Declare freedom, healing, joy, and peace in the mighty name of Jesus. Remember, the power of Christ is greater than the power of Satan, so do not fear! Stand against the stronghold of Jezebel, hold tightly to victory, and do not be denied!

There is no doubt that it is wise to be selective when it comes to which church body we choose to attend. This may require attending different churches for a while, so we can best decide which church home God may be calling us to. The goal is to find a church that teaches the Bible, which is the inerrant Word of God and affirms all of the essentials of the Christian faith. This may take some time and might technically be called church-hopping. However, after having found a solid church, we must commit to remaining there.

TEN THINGS CHURCH HOPPERS AND PROPHECY SHOPPERS WILL SAY

In my craving to find out why men and women of today's Christianity hop around prophets and pastors for quick fixes to their problems and seek favourable prophecies, I came across a book written by Bob Franquiz entitled, *Zero to Sixty*. In one of the chapters, Bob wrote ten things church hoppers say when they cannot find what they want from one church or another. I borrow some of his words in elaborating my facts.

1. "But my old church or this pastor…" This usually means they want your church to be like their old church or the pastor they are luring others to meet dances to their tune.

2. "I just need time to be fed or told something positive." This means, "I don't want to do anything. I'm here just to sit and see what I can get out of this church or the pastor, so don't expect me to serve in any way, shape or form."

3. "I'm looking for a church or a pastor that teaches the Word or tells me what I want to hear." This means, "I'm looking for a church or a pastor that dispenses lots of information without challenging me to do anything even though he/she knows I am sinning."

4. "I came here because I am looking for deep teaching on my prosperity." This usually means that their last pastor focused too much on obeying the Word of God. They want a church or pastor that just talks about their prosperity, their giving and self praises, who the Hittites were and the identity of Theophilus.

5. "I should know my pastor." This means they are using familiarity to disrespect their pastor. "I got to know the pastor but when the church grew, and the pastor couldn't have time for me, I left and sought another whom I think is more powerful than this one."

6. "I want a church or a pastor that's focused on discipling people." This means, "I want a church or a pastor that's focused on me, not people who are lost" (self-centeredness).

7. "This pastor doesn't seem to like me." This means they don't like commitment; they don't like to be told the Bible tells them how to live and follow Jesus. They want to come to church, live in their sins and have no one tell them this is wrong.

8. "I only want to talk to the pastor, not his wife." This is the best way to tell a pastor "I don't give a dam about your wife." Well, if you disrespect the pastor's wife you are disrespecting the pastor himself, and it's a curse.

9. "My old church/pastor was…" The way people come to your church is how they will leave. If your first conversation with them is all about their last church and pastor, that is how they will leave your church and how they will go to their next church and pastor seeking prayers and words of knowledge.

10. "Pastor, I've been talking to a lot of people and they all say…" Translation: "Me, my spouse and my mother think…" If they start this way, 99.9% of the time they have no one else who thinks this way. It is just the best way to complain. If someone has a complaint and uses this line with me, they need to list all the names or my best assumption is they talked to the same person 10 times.

In conclusion, if you know people who are church or prophecy shoppers consulting every pastor for prayers and prophecies, please pray for them. They need deliverance. If you draw near to God, He will draw near to you and will show you things that you do not know (Jeremiah 33:3). This is God's telephone number. Call Him today. He will answer you. Cast your load unto Jesus, He will carry it. Pray without ceasing. Don't be a lazy Christian.

Notes

CHAPTER 7

Understanding the Anointing

- What is the anointing?
- What does it mean to be anointed?
- What is the purpose of the anointing today (the anointing today and the anointing of Jesus Christ)?
- Do witches have anointing oil?
- How do we discern false anointing on people?

Question: "What is the anointing? What does it mean to be anointed?"

Answer: The origin of anointing comes from a practice of shepherds. Lice and other insects would often get into the wool of sheep. When they got near the sheep's head, they could burrow into the sheep's ears and kill them. So ancient shepherds poured oil on the sheep's head. This made the wool slippery, making it impossible for insects to get near the sheep's ears because the insects would slide off. From this, anointing became symbolic of blessing, protection, and empowerment.

The New Testament Greek words for "anoint" are *chrio*, which means "to smear or rub with oil" and, by implication, "to consecrate for office or religious service" and *aleipho*, which means "to anoint." In Bible times, people were anointed with oil to signify God's blessing or call on their lives (Exodus 29:7; Exodus 40:9; 2 Kings 9:6; Ecclesiastes 9:8; James 5:14). All these passages speak about God's instructions to anoint people. A person was anointed for a special purpose, e.g. to be a king, a prophet, a builder, etc. There is nothing wrong with anointing a person with oil today. We just have to make sure that the purpose of anointing is in agreement with Scripture. Anointing should not be viewed as a "magic potion." The oil itself does not have any power. It is only God who can anoint a person for a specific purpose. If we use oil, it is only a symbol of what God is doing.

Another meaning for the word "anointed" is "chosen one." The Bible says that Jesus Christ was anointed by God with the Holy Spirit to spread the good news and free those who have been held captive by sin (Luke 4:18-19; Acts 10:38). After Christ left the earth, He gave us the gift of the Holy Spirit (John 14:16). Now all Christians are anointed and chosen for a specific purpose in furthering God's kingdom (1 John 2:20). "Now He who establishes us with you in Christ and has anointed us is God, who also has sealed us and given us the Spirit in our hearts as a guarantee" (2 Corinthians 1:21-22).

ANOINTINGS TODAY

God is still anointing prophets today. Prophets are spokesmen for Him. The prophetic office includes anything that speaks for God—which would be all of the teaching and preaching offices—but especially that of the prophet because that is the anointing involved. God is still anointing people to preach, testify, and sing. And He's still anointing priests. What was the function of the priest? He represented other people. Other people couldn't go into the presence of God in the Holy of Holies, but the priest, the high priest could go into the Holy of Holies. He was the intercessor for the people. God is still anointing intercessors. He's anointing people to pray. There's an anointing there. And He's anointing kings. We're all kings, glory to God. Romans 5:17 says that we shall "reign in life." It's because of the anointing that we're able to reign. Other Old Testament references to the anointing include this text from Zechariah.

> Then he answered and spake unto me, saying, this is the word of the Lord unto Zerubbabel, saying, Not by might [or army], nor by power, but by my spirit, saith the Lord of hosts. (Zechariah 4:6)

We always think of might and power in connection with the Spirit of God. When God speaks of might and power in this Scripture, He's talking about human might. He's telling Zerubbabel, "It's not by the power of an army, but it's by my Spirit that the battle is going to be won." It's by the Spirit of God that victories come, not by the hand of man.

> And it shall come to pass in that day, that his burden shall be taken away from off thy shoulder, and his yoke from off thy neck, and the yoke shall be destroyed because of the anointing (Isaiah 10:27).

Sometimes we turn that phrase around and say, "It's the anointing that destroys (or breaks) the yoke." That's saying absolutely the same thing: The yoke shall be destroyed because of the anointing. This is true in our lives and ministries as well: the yoke of sickness or anything else the Devil tries to put on us will be destroyed because of the anointing. In the New Testament, we see how the anointing was on the ministry of Jesus, and we can learn about ministering under the anointing.

The Anointing on Jesus

> 14 And Jesus returned in the power of the spirit into Galilee: and there went out a fame of him through all the region round about. 15 And he taught in their synagogues, being glorified of all. (Notice in the fourteenth verse, the word "power" is used in connection with the Holy Spirit. Combining these two verses, we could say, "He returned in the power of the Spirit and He taught," or, "He taught in the power of the Spirit" (for there is an anointing to teach).
>
> 16 And he came to Nazareth, where he had been brought up: and, as his custom was, he went into the synagogue on the sabbath day, and stood up for to read. 17 And there was delivered unto him the book of the prophet Esaias [Isaiah]. And when he had opened the book, he found the place where it was written, 18 The Spirit of the Lord is upon me, because he hath anointed me to preach the gospel to the poor;

he hath sent me to heal the broken hearted, to preach deliverance to the captives, and recovering of sight to the blind, to set at liberty them that are bruised, 19 To preach the acceptable year of the Lord. Notice in connection with the Holy Spirit there first was the word "power" (v. 14) and then the word "anointed" (v. 18). (Luke 4:14-19)

Another example we could draw here is Peter. Preaching to Cornelius and his household, he said, "How God anointed Jesus of Nazareth with the Holy Ghost and with power: who went about doing good and healing all that were oppressed of the devil; for God was with him" (Acts 10:38).

Jesus said, "The Spirit of the Lord is upon me, because he hath anointed me" (Luke 4:18). God anointed Jesus primarily to do two things according to this entire verse: to preach and to heal. In connection with preaching, Jesus also was anointed to teach. If people would just stop and think for a moment, they would see this in Luke Chapter 4. Jesus was in His hometown of Nazareth on the Sabbath day. He went to the synagogue and was given the scroll of Isaiah to read from. He read: "The Spirit of the Lord is upon me, because he hath anointed me..." After He had finished reading, Jesus handed the scroll back to the minister, sat down, and began to teach the people. He said, "This day is this scripture fulfilled in your ears" (Luke 4:21).

If Jesus had been ministering as the Son of God, He wouldn't have needed to be anointed. Or, if He had been ministering as God manifested in the flesh, would God have needed to be anointed? Who is going to anoint God?

In Philippians 2:7, it says that Jesus "made himself of no reputation and took upon him the form of a servant and was made in the likeness of men." The King James Version is a little unclear here. Other translations say He "laid aside" or "stripped Himself" of "His mighty power and glory" when He came into this world, even though He was the Son of God. Now, think of how many people are looking for fame today in the name of a man who made Himself of no reputation and even became a servant to mankind. He came as a man. How did He do it? I don't know. The Bible says He did it, and I believe it!

As I've said many times, Jesus was just as much the Son of God when He was 21 years old as He was when He was 30 years old. He was just as much the Son of God when He was 25 as He was when He was 30. He was just as much the Son of God all those years 25, 26, 27, 28, 29, wasn't He? Yet, in all those years, people still doubt that He ever healed a person or wrought a miracle! How do we know this? Because the Bible says so. The Bible tells us that Jesus was anointed after He was baptized of John in Jordan, and the Holy Spirit came upon Him in a bodily shape like a dove (Luke 3:22). God spoke from heaven and said, "This is my beloved Son, in whom I am well pleased" (Matthew 3:17).

What is the purpose of the anointing today? (The anointing today and the anointing of Jesus Christ)

In conclusion, here are seven facts and purposes of the anointing and what the anointing will do in your life if you remain faithful in the Lord. We live in a day that is filled with both unthinkable peril and unimaginable opportunity. And if ever there was a time in history when the body of Christ needed God's anointing power, it is now! But what is the anointing, how do you move into it and how do you see it increase? The anointing is the overflow of Christ in your life! It comes to us as we spend time in God's Word, seek Him with our whole heart, and worship Him. Jesus said: "If ye abide in me, and my words abide in you, ye shall ask what ye will, and it shall be done unto you" (John 15:7). We increase the anointing by spending time in His presence. You will certainly know when the presence of the Holy Spirit has come upon your life.

THE SEVEN THINGS THE ANOINTING WILL DO FOR YOU. THESE ARE ABIDING PROMISES [16].

1. **Healing**. Just like when the good Samaritan ministered to the man who had been robbed, stripped, and left for dead (Luke 10:33-34), the minute God's anointing starts to flow on you, it will heal you. Your heart will be healed. He will restore your health.

---

[16] Pastor Derik Prince healing and deliverance ministries

And you will become a minister of His healing power. That is promised in God's Word.

2. **Revelation**. The anointing will change your life. Exodus 25:6 talks about the oil that brings light. It pierces the darkness and illuminates everything around it. Nothing can stop it because the anointing is the overflow of Christ's life. And once the anointing starts to flow over you, it brings revelation knowledge, allowing you to move into a supernatural walk with God.

3. **Provision.** In 1 Kings 17:14, we read about Elijah and the widow of Zarephath. She desperately needed a miracle. All she had left for herself and her son was a handful of meal and a small amount of oil. God performed a life-changing miracle for her, multiplying her offering far beyond anything she could have dreamed. The oil did not fail. And today, when God moves in your life, the oil begins to flow, meeting every need in your life. There will be no lack. That's what God wants for you today. He is moving mightily upon the earth—as you seek Him with your whole heart, the oil will flow on you, and every need in your life will be met!

4. **Debt-free living**. A widow came to Elisha and cried out about the debts that had overtaken her and her sons after her husband's death (2 Kings 4:1-7). God used all she had: a pot of oil—it

multiplied supernaturally, and she was able to pay off all her debts!

5. **Deliverance.** David spoke of the oil of anointing (Psalm 23:1-5) and how it delivered him from all his enemies. Not only that, but he also spoke of God's faithfulness in protecting him when he wrote, "Surely goodness and mercy shall follow me all the days of my life: and I will dwell in the house of the Lord forever."

6. **Faith.** We are told that the watchman of Isaiah 21:5 was directed to anoint the shield. Just as oil was used then, the oil of God's anointing must be used today. Faith must be activated and released, then God will protect you with the shield of faith because of that anointing. Today, regardless of your circumstances, He wants to release a mighty anointing on your life to protect you, completely and totally, but you must first activate it!

7. **Blessings.** Psalm 133 speaks about the precious oil of anointing that flowed over Aaron, then God directed the high priest to command His blessings: "The Lord commanded the blessing, even life for evermore" (Psalm 133:3) upon the children of Israel. Today, He commands the blessings on you through His Word. He even says, "All the promises of God in him are yea, and in him Amen, unto the glory of God by us" (2 Corinthians 1:20).

Every one of these seven promises of His anointing are for us today, to the glory of God!

God's Eternally Secure Promises.

The Word of God is God Himself; therefore, the Word of God cannot be broken. For God to break His Word would break God Himself. That's impossible! God cannot lie. That's why Jesus said it's easier for heaven and earth to pass away than for one dot to be removed from the Word of God (Matthew 5:18). God's Word is established forever. God said, "I am the Lord, I change not" (Malachi 3:6). It's His covenant to us. The anointing is the power to serve God. Throughout history, God has placed His anointing on people just like you and me whom He's used to do mighty things. When the anointing or the overflow of Christ comes on your life, it gives you the power to change lives and influence nations.

7.1 Do Witches Have Anointing Oil?

Yes, witches do have different types of anointing oils and anointing materials that range from colored candle sticks to perfumes. One of the articles written by Avalon Cameron [17] titled "Peri protection Spells" Cameron stated:

---

[17] Avalon Cameron (2017) titled "Peri protection Spells" p33

Understanding the Anointing

The Peries are Persian Faeries born from fire. They only eat perfume and are known to protect people against harmful faeries. In this spell, you are invoking the energy of the Peries as a means of protection from dark energies and negative events. You will need a green candle and three drops of jasmine-scented oil. Begin by anointing the candle with the three drops of oil while saying: "Blessed oil of jasmine sweet Draw the magick of the Peries to me." Then the candle is put in its holder, and light it while dedicating it to the Peris: "Born from the divine fire, Peries protect me from evil and darkness.

As I will, so shall it be!" the candle is now left to burn safely down all the way. Put some perfume on a piece of cloth and leave it out for the Peries. Anytime you feel darkness and negativity trying to come into your space, light a candle and call in the Peries for protection. Witches use the following tools; Spell Oils, Essential Oils, Anointing Oils and scented candles.

Spell oils are useful for many different purposes. You can find spell oils for anointing your tools and altar, focusing and enhancing your magickal intent during spells and rituals, drawing and sending, anointing your house and car for protection, and your person toward a specific intent as well as for pretty much every other purpose under the sun and moon. If you need a spell oil it probably already exists somewhere in the world. If not, you can learn to craft your own online in any number of reputable places or through the writings of reputable Witch authors.

What a myth. Can this nonsense protect people? No! Only Jesus Christ is the answer to human protection (Psalm 23, Psalm 27, and Psalm 121).

How do we discern false anointing on people?

> When a prophet speaketh in the name of the LORD, if the thing follows not, nor come to pass, that is the thing which the LORD hath not spoken, but the prophet hath spoken it presumptuously: thou shalt not be afraid of him. (Deuteronomy 18:22)

The inability to discern a false prophet from a true prophet will open the way for the deception of the false prophet (the Devil's evangelists) "out of the earth" (Revelation 13:11) who is the end time co-worker of the antichrist. All the marks of a false prophet should be understood by the body of believers and applied to our daily discernment of who ought to be believed and who ought to be rejected.

> For everyone that useth milk is unskillful in the Word of Righteousness: for he is a babe. But Strong Meat belongeth to them that are of full age, even those who by reason of use have their

senses exercised to discern both good and evil. (Hebrews 5:13-14, KJV)

Our LORD did not excuse the hypocrites for their lack of discerning the "signs of the times" (Matthew 16:3). He will also not excuse the world for allowing the false prophets to deceive them into worshipping the Antichrist. "And he [the false prophet] exerciseth all the power of the first beast [the Antichrist] before him, and causeth the Earth and them which dwell therein to worship the first beast, whose deadly wound was healed" (Revelation 13:12). Then, why should the Lord allow those of us who name the "name of Christ" (2Timothy 2:19) to be ignorant of the false prophets, who are currently deceiving the "flock of God" (1Peter 5:2)? Think about it.

Tom Stewart [18] a wonderful writer stated the following in his articles on discerning false prophets:

> A "prophet, or a dreamer of dreams", who gives a "sign or wonder" (Deut; 13:1) recalls the signs the LORD gave to Moses to convince the Children of Israel that Moses was truly sent from God-- turning Moses' rod into a serpent and back again (Exodus 4:2-4), and turning Moses' hand leprous and back again (4:6-8).

---

[18] Tom Stewart; (What saith the scriptures), This man has written articles on discerning false prophets and gave a biblical reference to help believers understand the intricacies of spiritual anointing and false anointing.

(Exodus 4:1, 9). "And Moses answered and said, But, behold, they [the Children of Israel] will not believe me, nor hearken unto my voice: for they will say, The LORD hath not appeared unto thee... 9 And it shall come to pass, if they will not believe also these two signs [the rod into a serpent, and the leprous hand], neither hearken unto thy voice, that thou shalt take of the water of the river, and pour it upon the dry land: and the water which thou takest out of the river shall become blood upon the dry land" and in (Deuteronomy 13:2). It says; "And the sign or the wonder come to pass, whereof he spake unto thee, saying, Let us go after other gods, which thou hast not known, and let us serve them;" We are not to think it strange that even a false prophet can make the "sign or the wonder come to pass" (13:2) by the supernatural power of Satan. "For there shall arise false Christs, and false prophets, and shall shew great signs and wonders; insomuch that, if it were possible, they shall deceive the very elect" **(Matthew 24:24).** Of course, the Almighty must first give permission to Satan before Satan has the slightest ability to accomplish anything. Or, as the LORD Jesus plainly explained to Pontius Pilate concerning the limit of Pilate's control over Himself: "you would have no power at all against Me, except it were given to you from above (John 19:11).

Pivotal to the concept of identifying false prophets, is that a false prophet seeks to turn people away from the LORD Jesus Christ, i.e., "Let us go after other gods, which thou hast not known, and let us serve them" (Deuteronomy 13:2). If we understand that our loving obedience to the Word of God is the basis for our certainty that we belong to Him, then we also know that anyone who is clearly in disobedience to the commands of our LORD Jesus Christ, is a liar.

"3 And hereby we do know that we know Him, if we keep His Commandments. 4 He that saith, I know Him, and keepeth not His Commandments, is a liar, and the Truth is not in Him" (1John 2:3-4). "Thou shalt not hearken unto the words of that prophet, or that dreamer of dreams: for the LORD your God proveth you, to know whether ye love the LORD your God with all your heart and with all your soul" (Deuteronomy 13:3).

Finally, I would like to call on those who want to partner with this Ministry, as this is an exciting and thrilling hour! We are seeing an intensity of the anointing and the power of God in our ministry that I have not seen in decades. And at the same time, I'm seeing a hunger among the lost and hurting for the peace that only salvation through Jesus Christ can bring. Truly, God is on the move, and I want you to be part of all God is doing right now. If you are so blessed by all these teachings and messages, please call us today on +614 0512 5759 and partner with us so we can reach those that are hungry and thirsty for the Word of God. Nothing is too small or large to offer. Be blessed. Graceministries2017@gmail.com

Notes

CHAPTER 8

What Does the Bible Teach Us About Giving?

BIBLE TEACHINGS ABOUT GIVING

a) What does the Bible say about giving?

b) What are the types of giving the Bible and church preachers spoke about?

c) What did Jesus and His ministry teach about giving?

And he blessed Abram, saying, "Blessed be Abram by God Most High, Creator of heaven and earth. 20 And praise be to God Most High, who delivered your enemies into your hand." Then Abram gave him a tenth of everything. (Genesis 14:19-20).

(Please note here: Abram gives Melchizedek a tenth of his spoils, but there is no command to do so. It's motivated by Abram's love for God and his conviction that Melchizedek is God's special servant.)

Made a vow, saying, "If God will be with me and will watch over me on this journey I am taking and will give me food to eat and clothes to wear 21 so that I return safely to my father's household, then the

LORD will be my God 22 and this stone that I have set up as a pillar will be God's house, and of all that you give me I will give you a tenth. (Genesis 28:20-22)

(Exodus 25:2; 35:5; 36:5-7; Leviticus 27:30-34; Numbers 18:21-26)

But you are to seek the place the LORD your God will choose from among all your tribes to put his Name there for his dwelling. To that place you must go; 6 there bring your burnt offerings and sacrifices, your tithes and special gifts, what you have vowed to give and your freewill offerings, and the firstborn of your herds and flocks. (Deuteronomy 12:5-6)

We also assume responsibility for bringing to the house of the LORD each year the first fruits of our crops and of every fruit tree. 36 "As it is also written in the Law, we will bring the firstborn of our sons and of our cattle, of our herds and of our flocks to the house of our God, to the priests ministering there. 37 "Moreover, we will bring to the storerooms of the house of our God, to the priests, the first of our ground meal, of our grain offerings, of the fruit of all our trees and of our new wine and olive oil. And we will bring a tithe of our crops to the Levites, for it is the Levites who collect the tithes in all the towns where we work. (Nehemiah 10:35-37)

He ordered the people living in Jerusalem to give the portion due the priests and Levites so they could devote themselves to the Law of the

LORD. 5 As soon as the order went out, the Israelites generously gave the first fruits of their grain, new wine, olive oil and honey and all that the fields produced. They brought a great amount, a tithe of everything. (2 Chronicles 31:4-5)

Will a mere mortal rob God? Yet you rob me. "But you ask, 'How are we robbing you?'" "In tithes and offerings. 9 You are under a curse— your whole nation—because you are robbing me. 10 Bring the whole tithe into the storehouse, that there may be food in my house. Test me in this," says the LORD Almighty, "and see if I will not throw open the floodgates of heaven and pour out so much blessing that there will not be room enough to store it. 11 I will prevent pests from devouring your crops, and the vines in your fields will not drop their fruit before it is ripe," says the LORD Almighty. 12 "Then all the nations will call you blessed, for yours will be a delightful land," says the LORD Almighty. (Malachi 3:8-12)

NT Scriptures: Matthew 23:23; Mark 4:8; Luke 11:42; 2 Corinthians 9:6-12; Acts 2:44-47; Heb. 7:12; 2 Corinthians 8:1-12, and more.

INTRODUCTION

The question about giving to the church has raised a lot of concerns all over the world today. Many pastors and church leaders have used and are still using their places of worship as money-making machines leaving the congregation wondering why the same God has not opened the flood gates and windows of heaven to pour them their own blessings. In my quest to find answers, I realized these questions are pretty open-ended and could easily go in any number of directions. So, I want to focus on the issue of motivation. Why do we give? What is the purpose of giving? It should be no surprise that the answer is wonderfully simple and unimaginably complex, all at the same time.

I want to also endeavour to answer some of these questions

1. What does the Bible say about giving?

2. What types of giving does the Bible recognize?

3. What did Jesus and His ministry teach about the willingness to give believers and faithful givers an opportunity to further understand the reasons why they should or should not give?

For many of us, particularly those of us in the compassion world, it's really tempting to point and look at the needs of the world and say, "That's why we give. We're giving so we can bless others." This is a good motivation but biblically, it's not the starting place for God's people. We also have to remember that generosity is about so much more than money; it's about our entire lives giving of our time, talents, and treasures.

THE MESSAGE TO ANSWER THE QUESTIONS:
What does the Bible say about giving?

The Bible tells us that giving shows Jesus is Lord of our lives. First and foremost, God wants us to give because it shows that we recognize He is truly the Lord of our lives. Every good and perfect gift is from above, coming down from the Father of the heavenly lights, who does not change like shifting shadows (James 1:17, NIV). Everything we have comes from God. So when we give, we simply offer Him a small portion of the abundance He has already given to us.

Giving is an expression of our thankfulness and praise to God. It comes from a heart of worship that recognizes everything we have and give already belongs to the Lord. God instructed Old Testament believers to give a tithe or a tenth because this ten percent represented the first, most important portion of all they had. The New Testament does not suggest a certain percentage for giving but simply says for each to give "in keeping with his income." The New Testament never gives a certain percentage point as an obligatory and required standard for our giving. Instead, the Scriptures declare, "Let each one does just as he has purposed in his heart; not grudgingly or under compulsion; for God loves a cheerful giver" (2 Corinthians 9:7).

The Old Testament tithe was required by law. The Jews were under compulsion to give it. The New Testament teaching on giving focuses on its voluntary character. "For I testify that according to their ability, and beyond their ability they gave of their own accord" (2 Corinthians 8:3). This voluntary giving is exactly what Abraham and Jacob were doing before the institution of the Law and is what all Christians are to be doing today. Believers today are free to give the amount they choose to give. If they want to give ten per cent as Abraham and Jacob did. They are perfectly free to do so. However, if they decide to give 9, 11, 20 or 50 per cent, then they may do that as well. Their standard of giving is not a fixed percentage point but the example of their wonderful Saviour, "For you know the grace of our Lord Jesus Christ, that though He was rich, yet for your sake He became poor, that you through His poverty might become rich" (2 Corinthians 8:9).

b) What are the types of giving the Bible and church preachers spoke about?

What's fascinating is that this is the pattern throughout the Bible: God's grace motivates generosity in His people for the purpose of glorifying God. The Bible distinguishes between 4 different kinds of giving, each with a different purpose, motivation, and reward for you to expect in return. It is vitally important for you to understand the difference between them before you start giving because a full understanding and an application of the four different types will help you get your whole financial life under control.

Each type of giving should be practiced with the right motivation and correct understanding of the reward. Your heart's attitude is what matters here. In the Old and New Testaments, the Bible and prosperity gospel preachers distinguish the following kinds of giving;

1. TITHING (10%) — Malachi 3, 8-11

Here the motivation is simply obedience and the reward is the blessing. Therefore, it is my conviction that the blessings and curses spoken of in Malachi 3:8-12 refer to the material blessings God promised to Israel if she would obey His commandments and statutes. Tithing was one such commandment.

What can we conclude, therefore, about tithing under the Mosaic Law? I think we can safely conclude that tithing had nothing to do with the regular giving of money on a weekly or monthly basis. Rather, it had to do with the ordained worship of God in the Old Covenant age. The command to tithe, like the command not to eat shrimp or oysters, has been made obsolete and set aside by the inauguration of the New Covenant in the death of Christ. The tithe was God's ordained tax under the Old Testament theocratic system. In Matthew 23:23, Jesus said "Woe to you, scribes and Pharisees, hypocrites! For you tithe mint and dill and cumin and have neglected the weightier provisions of the law: justice and mercy and faithfulness; but these are the things you should have done without neglecting the others."

In this passage in Matthew, which is also repeated in similar fashion in Luke 11:42, it is important to notice that the tithe had to do with garden herbs (the product of the field) rather than with money. Additionally, Jesus spoke these words to very religious, law-keeping Pharisees while the Mosaic Law was still in force. To say that since Jesus told these Pharisees it was right for them to tithe, thus, it is right for us to tithe as well, misses the fact that these Pharisees lived under a different covenant with different laws than the New Testament believer does. By Christ's death, He inaugurated the New Covenant, thereby bringing about a change in the law (Luke 22:20; Hebrews 7:12). Finally, notice that the tithe mentioned here was not voluntary in any sense of the word. Jesus tells them that they *"ought" to have tithed. (Past tense).* It was obligatory on all Jews and thus binding. And if that's the case, our giving has to be motivated by something far greater than need.

2. THE SEED (Mark 4:2-8)

The phrase "sowing seeds" is use often in the church, especially among prosperity gospel and word of faith preachers. When they use the phrase, they are referring to you giving money to their ministry. When they talk about tithing, they are also referring to you giving money to their ministry. What does the Bible say about sowing seeds and tithing? Are they the same? Are preachers in error when they tell you to sow seeds? Is sowing seeds replacing the practice of so-called tithing? Why is there so much emphasis placed on sowing seeds (i.e., giving your money to a preacher, church or ministry)?

Let's talk about what the church doesn't want you to talk about. In today's church, tithing and sowing seeds both refer to money. However, the Bible does not equate tithing and sowing seeds with money. According to the Bible, tithing, sowing seeds, and money are not the same.

The tithe is explained above. The biblical tithe refers to 10 percent of agricultural produce and livestock grown in the land of ancient Israel. When preachers tell you that tithing means you should give money, they are incorrect.

Sowing Seeds — The word "seed" and the term "sowing seeds" are often used to refer to money, especially in the prosperity gospel and word of faith movements. This was a topic I dealt with some time ago on our WhatsApp forum making things very clear that prosperity gospel preachers and the word of faith movements are bent on milking you dry whilst they are flying jets and driving expensive cars at your own expense. As said earlier, but worthy of repeating, the Bible speaks of seeds or sowing seeds in two ways. First, the word "seed" or phrase "sowing seeds" is a reference to farming or agriculture. Specifically, planting seeds in the ground for the purpose growing food, plants, trees, flowers, etc. (Genesis 1:11). Second, the phrase "sowing seeds" is used as a metaphor. A metaphor is a figure of speech used to compare two unlike things that actually have something in common. Examples of metaphors: Life is like a box of chocolates, skin like silk.

Jesus uses "seed" and "sowing seeds" as a metaphor in His seed parable (Matthew 13:1-58, Mark 4:2-41). Is Jesus talking about money? Absolutely not! See Luke 8:11. The word "seed" is a metaphor for the Word of God. The word "sow" is a metaphor for sharing, speaking and/or teaching the Word of God.

Ground/soil is a metaphor for the heart. Jesus never uses the words "sowing seeds" as a metaphor for giving money. For a detailed teaching on the seed parable, please read *Exposing the Seed Faith Doctrine* written by R. Renee and Cynthia Harper. It's on Amazon.

Preachers and Sowing Seeds — Many preachers commonly use "sowing seeds" as a metaphor for money. They are not wrong to use it as a metaphor for money. Sowing seeds may be used as a metaphor for anything. For example, a seed can be wisdom, encouragement, gratitude, or a compliment. In other words, you can sow a seed of wisdom, encouragement, and gratitude into someone's life. The problem with preachers constantly associating sowing seeds with money is that it leads you to believe the Bible is always referring to money when you see the word "seed" or "sowing seeds" in the scriptures. Generally speaking, the Bible does not use seed or sowing seeds as a metaphor for money.

3. The First Fruit Giving — First fruits giving was a Jewish feast held in the early spring at the beginning of the grain harvest. It was observed on Nissan 16, which was the third day after Passover and the second day of the Feast of Unleavened Bread. First fruits giving was a time of thanksgiving for God's provision. The Levites instituted first fruits offering in Leviticus 23:9-14. The people were to bring a sheaf of grain to the priest, who would wave it before the Lord. A burnt offering, a meal offering, and a drink offering were also required at that time. Deuteronomy 26:1-10 gives even more details on the procedure of first fruits.

No grain was to be harvested at all until the first fruits offering was brought to the Lord (Leviticus 23:14). The offering was made in remembrance of Israel's sojourn in Egypt, the Lord's deliverance from slavery, and their possession of "a land that floweth with milk and honey."

The day of the first fruits offering was also used to calculate the proper time of the Feast of Weeks (Leviticus 23:15-16).

In the New Testament, the first fruits offering is mentioned seven times, which is always symbolical. Paul calls Epaenetus and the household of Stephanas "the first fruits of Achaia" (Romans 16:5; 1 Corinthians 16:15). His meaning is that, just as the first fruits offering was the first portion of a larger harvest, these individuals were the first of many converts in that region. James calls believers "a kind of first fruits of His creatures" (James 1:18). Just like the sheaf of grain was set apart for the Lord, so are believers set apart for God's glory.

The first fruits offering found its fulfillment in Jesus. "But Christ has indeed been raised from the dead, the first fruits of those who have fallen asleep" (1 Corinthians 15:20). Jesus' resurrection has paved the way for our resurrection. Significantly, if Jesus was killed at Passover, then His resurrection on the third day would have fallen on Nissan 16 the Feast of First fruits. The first fruits offering is never directly applied to Christians giving in the New Testament. However, Paul taught the Corinthian believers to set aside a collection "on the first day of the week" (1 Corinthians 16:2). And, just as the offering of first fruits was an occasion of thanksgiving, so the Christian is to give with gladness.

In summary, first fruits symbolize God's harvest of souls. It illustrates giving to God from a grateful heart and sets a pattern of giving back to

Him the first (and the best) of what He has given us. Not being under the Old Testament Law, the Christian is under no further obligation than to give cheerfully and liberally (2 Corinthians 9:6-7).

4. ALMS GIVING — Alms are money or goods given to those in need as an act of charity. The word "alms" is used many times in the King James Version of the Bible. It comes from the Old English word **æ**lmesse and ultimately from a Greek word meaning "pity, mercy." In its original sense, when you give alms, you are dispensing mercy. Almsgiving is a long-standing practice within the Judeo-Christian tradition. "Whoever is kind to the needy honours God" (Proverbs 14:31; see also Proverbs 19:17; 21:13; 22:9 and 29:7). Jesus and His disciples gave money to the poor (John 12:6). Believers are to "remember the poor" (Galatians 2:10). The godly Tabitha was praised as one who was continually "helping the poor" (Acts 9:36).

The word "alms" is used nine times in five chapters of the King James Version of the New Testament. Matthew 6:1-4 contains four occurrences:

> Take heed that ye do not your alms before men, to be seen of them: otherwise ye have no reward of your Father which is in heaven. Therefore, when thou doest thine alms, do not sound a trumpet before thee, as the hypocrites do in the synagogues and in the streets, that they may have glory of men. Verily I say unto you, they have their reward. But when thou doest alms, let not thy left hand know what thy right hand doeth: That thine alms may be in secret:

and thy Father which seeth in secret himself shall reward thee openly.

Here, Jesus taught that almsgiving is for God to see, not to show off before others. Those giving out of their love for God are not to announce their giving or draw attention to it. In Luke 11:40-42, Jesus rebukes the Pharisees for giving alms but "neglecting justice and the love of God." In other words, these religious leaders gave to charity; yet, they did not have true charity in their hearts. Giving to the needy does not necessarily prove a right relationship with God.

In Luke 12:32, Jesus tells a rich young ruler to sell all he had, give alms to the poor, and follow Him. Jesus' challenge was meant to reveal where the young man's devotion was: did he love money more than the Lord? The man turned and walked away from Jesus, unwilling to part with his fortune. Doing so showed that he was not ready to become a disciple.

In Acts 3, a crippled man asked Peter and John for money. The apostles explained that they had no money, and they healed him instead. This miracle was much greater than any alms they could have given! Biblically, giving financially to those in need is an important expression of the Christian faith. However, we should make sure our giving is done out of a true love for God, without drawing attention to ourselves. When we invest what God has given us to impact the lives of others, we can trust that the results will make a difference both now and for eternity.

Giving is meant to be a joyful expression of thanks to God from the heart, not a legalistic obligation. The value of our offering is not determined by *how much* we give but *how* we give.

Before I conclude, I should also throw light on the difference between faith offering and free will offering. As I mentioned earlier, giving should be a joyful expression of our thanks to God, not someone coming to tell us what to give and how to give.

What is a freewill offering?

The free will (or freewill) offering was a sacrifice regulated by God's standards in the Mosaic Law, but it was completely voluntary (Leviticus 23:38). In the Law, the free will offering was to be of a male bull, sheep or goat with no physical deformities or blemishes, and it was not to have been purchased from a foreigner (Leviticus 22:17–25). The offering was to include flour mixed with oil and wine; the amounts varied on whether the sacrifice was a lamb, bull, or ram (Numbers 15:1–10). As with all sacrifices, the free will offering was to be made in a place of God's choosing, not in an area formerly used by other religions or at home (Deuteronomy 12).

Although it was appropriate to give the sacrifice during formal feast-days, it could be given any time (Deuteronomy 16:10). Unlike other offerings governed by stricter rules, the priests could eat the free will offering on the day it was sacrificed or the day after (Leviticus 7:16–18).

Free will offerings did not always have to be animals, grain or drink offerings. The first time a free will offering is mentioned in the Bible is in Exodus 35:10–29. God had given instructions on how to build the tabernacle, and Moses relayed what supplies were needed for its construction. The people responded as their hearts stirred them, bringing jewelry, fine yarn, tanned skins, silver, bronze, acacia wood, onyx stones, spices, and oil. These items were all donated "as a freewill offering to the Lord" (Exodus 35:29).

Centuries later, the people made similar offerings for David to pass on to Solomon to build the temple (1 Chronicles 9:1–9). In the book of Ezra, the people gave traditional animal offerings, (Ezra 3:5) as well as supplies to rebuild the temple after the Babylonian captivity (Ezra 2:68; 7:16; 8:28). The people also made animal offerings in 2 Chronicles 31 when King Hezekiah, one of Judah's best kings, led the nation in returning to God and reinstituting His ceremonies. In Ezekiel 46:12, free will offerings are mentioned as being offered in the millennial kingdom. This form of giving is instructive and requires perfection.

FAITH GIVING, on the other hand is motivated by conviction and led by the Holy Spirit through compassion. It does not break you but stretches you to the limit. I share with you a story of how I attended a school of intercessors, and we were asked to do a faith offering. As a pastor, I thought giving at least one third of what I had would have been sufficient but alas, as I was coming back from putting what I thought was my faith offering, a small voice came into my ears saying, "Go back and put everything or every penny you have in your wallet" Wow! This was now a conviction by the Lord that I should be obedient. Faith giving is to be totally available and radically obedient. The Bible says, "Each of you should give what you have decided in your heart to give, not reluctantly or under compulsion, for God loves a cheerful giver" (2 Corinthians 9:7). Whenever we show our generosity through faith giving, we will absolutely prosper. Proverbs 11:25 says; "A generous person will prosper; whoever refreshes others will be refreshed."

Paul said that "For if the willingness is there, the gift is acceptable according to what one has, not according to what one does not have" (2 Corinthians 8:12). So let us take delight in the Lord, and he will give us the desires of our hearts (Psalm 37:4).

If this message has blessed you with knowledge and understanding of how to give, put God in first place in your heart and bless somebody financially, morally, spiritually or physically. God bless you for being a

An Introduction to Some Unanswered Questions In Christendom

blessing to our ministry. Please do not hesitate to call us on +614 0512 5759 or email us your questions, concerns and prayer request on graceministries2017@gmail.com . God bless you.

Be blessed for taking your time to read the thoughts of the men and women of God whose writings contributed a great deal to the completion of this book.

Notes

www.ingramcontent.com/pod-product-compliance
Lightning Source LLC
Chambersburg PA
CBHW032040290426
44110CB00012B/884